D1378339

This book is given to

_____

because I care about
your greater success.

From:

_____

To order bulk copies for
your team and clients, visit
STARTWITHYOURPEOPLE.COM.

Praise for

Start with Your People

Few people I know care for others better than Brian Dixon. In his book *Start with Your People*, he demonstrates how and why what matters most in life is the "who." Whether you're an employee or an entrepreneur, Brian will show you the path to putting people first and why it just might be the best way to do business.

JEFF GOINS, bestselling author of *The Art of Work*

Most people are obsessed with business growth. But Brian teaches how to focus on serving souls because in doing so you'll grow more than you can imagine! And fast. A must read for anyone looking to make a lasting impact and live an abundant, meaningful life.

SUSIE MOORE, tech start-up advisor and life coach

When I read Brian's admission that he's the least likely person to write this book, I laughed out loud, because he's right. But as a writer, I understand we don't often write about what comes easy. We write about the things we've had to struggle through, fight for, and learn the hard way. Over the last few years, I've had a front row seat to watch as Brian has pivoted from being project centric to people centric. With business savvy and a heart for helping people, his wisdom is hard-won, and it's an honor to call him a friend.

EMILY P. FREEMAN, *Wall Street Journal* bestselling author of *The Next Right Thing*

Business even twenty-five years ago required face-to-face contact. We met, had lunch, discussed family, and then conducted business. But now we have the technology to replace all that time-consuming personal contact. We look for the transaction before the relationship. We all want to "scale" and grow. Sears and Marshall Field's grew because of their attention to employees and customers and then disappeared into oblivion because their successful growth no longer allowed that personal service. Brian is a master of the technology of modern business. I trust him totally to create and manage the tools of my business. But he also understands the need to *Start with Your People*. This book gently reminds us to not forget the heart of our businesses even if our heads can open the door to impersonal growth.

DAN MILLER, *New York Times* bestselling
author and career transition coach

Brian Dixon is one of the most generous, consistent, and reliable humans I know. He has a passion for helping entrepreneurs flourish, thrive, and succeed. Whatever he's writing, read it. Your life and business will be all the better for it.

JEVONNAH "LADY J" ELLISON, author and high performance coach

In business you need three things to be successful: product, process, and people. And by far, people are most important. In *Start with Your People* Brian Dixon shows you how to put people first and in the process build a business filled with profit and purpose.

RYAN LEVESQUE, Inc. 500 CEO and national
bestselling author of *Ask* and *Choose*

Brian has figured out the key to any successful business. It isn't complicated; it always starts with *people*. Focusing on people. Loving on people. Serving people. This is the secret sauce of any successful business, and I love how Brian simplifies this so well in this book!

JENNIFER ALLWOOD, author and business coach

Everyone tries to check off lists and get things done on their way to success, but Brian Dixon knows something that few have figured out: it's all about people. This book will show you how the best ideas are brought to life through relationships.

BEN ARMENT, author of *Dream Year*

For years I've believed true leaders don't just solve problems. They also sit with people's pain. Brian Dixon's wonderful new book, *Start with Your People*, gives us actionable steps to go further and faster through the power of an engaged team.

KARY OBERBRUNNER, author of *Your Secret Name*, *The Deeper Path*, *Day Job to Dream Job*, and *Elixir Project*

Whether you are an employee or an entrepreneur, people are the key to a successful business. But the question is, "How do I run a business that puts people first?" That's why I love this book from Brian Dixon. He'll show you a path to purpose and profit—by putting people first!

CHANDLER BOLT, founder of Self-Publishing School, author of six books

Finally, a user manual for the people in your life! In *Start with Your People*, Brian Dixon offers a unique look into how to partner with people to accomplish your wildest dreams. People don't want to feel used; they want to feel appreciated. After reading this book, you'll have a newfound clarity of purpose, a plan for daily practice, and a clear path to profit.

JONATHAN MILLIGAN, BloggingYourPassion.com

Loving people and allowing your business to love people, to serve people, is life changing. It is life changing for your customers as they are able to see transformation happen in their lives with *your* products, and it is life changing for you as the business owner. It all comes down to your people. Start by finding your peeps! Brian is a genius at connecting people and helping businesses grow their impact and income. This book is a must-read!

RACHEL MILLER, founder of Moolah Marketing

If you've struggled to get your business off the ground, you're about to learn that everything changes when you shift your focus away from yourself and onto how you can serve those in your community. In *Start with Your People*, Brian will show you a path to purpose and profit.

CLIFF RAVENSCRAFT, business mentor and life coach at CliffRavenscraft.com

One of the most useful business books I've read in a long time. Brian nails it—the decision that changes everything is to start with your people. The ten characteristics Brian shares on page 72 should be required reading for all business people—and that's just *one page* in this amazing book. Buy it, read it, but, most importantly, act on it!

RAY EDWARDS, keynote speaker and bestselling author

For several years I've seen firsthand—and been amazed at—Brian's daily dedication and drive for others to succeed. This book is filled with how-tos for success and progress with family, friends, people, career, business, and life. It's straight-to-the-point and practical, with advice and take-aways on every page. Our efforts at progress impact everyone around us, and this book helps us impact them well and with purpose.

GARY MORLAND, cofounder of hope*writers

START
WITH YOUR
PEOPLE

THE DAILY DECISION THAT
CHANGES EVERYTHING

BRIAN DIXON

To you and the person you will become

ZONDERVAN

Start with Your People
Copyright © 2019 by Brian Dixon

Requests for information should be addressed to:
Zondervan, *3900 Sparks Dr. SE, Grand Rapids, Michigan 49546*

ISBN 978-0-310-35636-3 (hardcover)

ISBN 978-0-310-35777-3 (international trade paper edition)

ISBN 978-0-310-35657-8 (audio)

ISBN 978-0-310-35637-0 (ebook)

The author is represented by the literary agency of Alive Literary Agency, www .aliveliterary.com.

Cover design: Sangita Sutradhar
Cover image: elenabs / depositphotos
Interior design: Denise Froehlich

Printed in the United States of America

19 20 21 22 23   LSC   10 9 8 7 6 5 4 3 2 1

Contents

Foreword

In my early days as an entrepreneur, I had an experience that forever changed the way I approached both my business and the people around me.

In the fall of 2013, I attended a conference for online business owners. I was excited to be there but a little nervous because I felt *so* out of my league.

My business was still just getting started, and in my eyes, the speakers might as well have been rock stars. I was in awe.

At dinner on the first night of the conference, I was seated at a table with a couple of the speakers, one of whom I had been following for some time and was really excited to meet. At some point the discussion at the table turned to business. It was pretty lively, with some very different philosophies and passionate arguments from all sides. In the end, we all agreed to disagree.

Or so I thought.

As it turned out, these two speakers had other ideas. The next day, they chose their moment on stage as an opportunity to call me out and to mock my ideas. They did not name me but gave enough detail that it was clear to anyone who had been at the table who they were talking about.

They were the guys on stage, and I was just the nobody sitting in the audience. I had little choice other than to sit there and listen to them make fun of me.

At first I was mortified. Then I was angry. I tried to think of some way to get revenge, but of course I couldn't think of anything. But then, as I calmed down and the initial sting of embarrassment faded away, I began to feel sorry for them.

You see, these two guys seized an opportunity to put me down when they were already holding all the cards. I was nothing to them. They were the ones everyone was there to see.

Humiliating *me* only made them small.

On the flight home I replayed the scene at dinner over and over again in my head. I wondered what I could've done or said differently.

Ultimately, I realized that the problem was theirs, not mine.

And right there on that airplane, on the back of my napkin, I wrote down five simple reminders to myself:

Be humble.
Be kind.
Be generous.
Be encouraging.
Be forgiving.

It wasn't so much a set of goals as it was a creed, a motto for how to live my life and run my blog, a list of the five characteristics I most want to display to everyone I come across, five habits I wanted to instill in my life that year and every year.

I vowed that, no matter what, I would not be small in my business practices.

It was a lesson I will always be grateful for.

But at that conference, I got so much more than just a lesson in how to play big.

I got a lifelong friend.

You see, that *very same conference* is where I met Brian Dixon for the first time.

And Brian was anything but small.

Not only was he incredibly kind, he was exceedingly generous with both his encouragement and advice. We became friends, and over the years, as our entrepreneurship journeys paralleled one another, we'd run into each other here and there—sometimes online, sometimes at a conference or an event. I watched as he grew his business by pouring into people, by forging genuine connections, and by giving generously of his time and expertise. I noticed because those were the same qualities I had been striving to embody in my business as well.

A few years later, I decided the time was right to host my *own* conference for online business owners, which I called *Activate*. My goal was to create an event that would not only provide clear, cohesive, and actionable advice but also make every attendee feel welcomed, included, and encouraged.

Because the event's culture was so important to me, I only wanted to invite speakers that I knew personally, people I knew would be willing to give way more than they received, experts who would not only share their wisdom but pour into the attendees.

Brian's name was at the top of my list.

And let me just tell you—he could not have been more generous. Not only were his presentations among the highest rated talks at the event, but he also spent the rest of his time during those four days answering questions, giving feedback, and meeting with attendees one on one to provide guidance and advice. He even hosted an impromptu worship service on Sunday morning.

He didn't do any of it because he had to or because I asked him to.

He did it because that's who Brian is.

And that is what makes his message so incredibly powerful.

Every entrepreneur wants their business to succeed. Often we convince ourselves that it is a lack of strategy or a solid marketing plan that's holding us back. Maybe it's that we don't have the right advertising or the right budget or access to the right resources.

But the secret to success in both business and life is staring us right in the face.

Start with your people.

Whether it's your friends, your family, your team, or your customers, the people in your life are the greatest asset that you have. And that is true whether you are still just getting started, dreaming of making a change, or already on your way. All you need to do is learn how to leverage that asset.

This book will show you how to do that, and it was written by a person I am proud to call my friend, a person who has not only seen this work but actually lived it.

It's your guidebook to playing big, both in your business and in your life.

And every one of us needs to hear its message.

So soak it in, friend. Good stuff is coming your way!

xoxo,

Ruth Soukup, founder of Ruth Soukup
Omnimedia Inc. and *New York Times*
bestselling author of *Do It Scared*

CHAPTER 1

A Shocking Discovery
and a Resolution

I t was the hardest thing I've ever done in my life. Challenged
by a business coach to take my life and business to the next
level, I asked fifty-three friends, clients, and colleagues for their
honest feedback.

My coach called it a 360 Assessment, an anonymous survey
through which you get real, unfiltered feedback from key people in
your life. I called it terrifying. It's called a 360 Assessment because
it is supposed to include feedback from people all around you. They
tell your strengths, your weaknesses, and what they really think of
your personality, work ethic, and skills.

Imagine your former boss, coworker, or family member telling
you exactly what they think about you. Scary, right?

At first, I made a list of thirty friends, clients, coworkers, and
other people with whom I used to work. I started with people I
thought would have nice things to say; however, I realized that if
I honestly wanted to do this exercise well, I needed to ask people

who had something negative to say about me. People I had let down, disappointed, and though I hate to admit it, people who might have had a genuine concern. I searched through my email and found people whose projects hadn't worked out. A former boss, a few unhappy clients, the coaching student who never really took my advice. I reached out. They were sent a secret link to an anonymous survey in which they could tell their unfiltered truth about me. My strengths, my weaknesses, and the scariest box of all: "If you could tell Brian anything, what would you say?"

Over the next few days, I received twenty-six responses. What did people really think of me? I took a deep breath and started to read.

"I honestly like Brian as a person, but he's challenging to work with at times. He doesn't listen well, steamrolls over people, and he can wear a mask of charm and optimism which feels manipulative."

"He can prioritize tasks over people and not realize the bridges that are burning behind him. He can be unaware of his tone, of how he comes across when he's trying to make a point."

And then the real kicker. "Brian often puts projects over people."

These and other comments were sobering. Sure, I could have moped around, defended my position, justified my past actions, or given an excuse. But instead, working with my coach, I decided to do the hardest thing: face the truth.

I took a deep breath and made a decision. To move forward, I needed to make things right with the people I hurt. If I ever hoped to make a difference, to lead a life encouraging others to take full responsibility for themselves, I had to start with my people.

I wrote to a former contractor who didn't work out, a client with a misunderstanding, and a friend who had grown distant.

Here is an example of one of those emails.

Dear [Name],
Recently I completed a 360 Assessment and learned some hard things about myself. Looking back on our work together, I know

there are things I could have done differently and better. I take full responsibility and apologize for the way things worked out between us. I'm truly sorry. Would you forgive me?

Brian

After just a few minutes of waiting, I received my first response.

Of course, Brian! No problem. Thanks for thinking of me.

Wow! This was going to be easier than I thought.

Then it hit me: I hadn't done the hard work. More names came to mind, more emails to send. I dug deep into the archives. Those other email addresses I hadn't used for a year. More names, unresolved conflicts, and misunderstandings. Searching my heart, I continued to reach out to former colleagues and clients with whom I knew I could have done better. With each apology, there was a feeling of being set free. Owning my part and asking for forgiveness opened my heart toward each person. People were released from the grudge I was holding against them. In all, I sent thirty-two emails. Thirty-two difficult yet liberating emails.

Over the next few days, I heard back from almost every single person. They were gracious and they were kind. For most of these situations, I always meant to do the right thing, to follow up, finish the project, send the report, but I got busy and time moved on. The survey responders were right: I put projects over people. Instead of basking in the sunshine of my attention, they were left in the shadow of my neglect. I closed the door, slammed it right in their faces, and then blamed the wind.

You might assume that's the end of the story, right? Just put people first and everything turns out fine. I wish. For the next few months, I was on cloud nine. My business was growing, I had more confidence than ever before, and I was landing clients I'd never even been able to get on the phone.

Months later, I was speaking at a conference, really in my zone, throwing down some truth from the stage and amping people up. When I got off the stage, I recognized a former client I hadn't spoken with in quite some time. She'd paid a fifteen-hundred-dollar deposit, but the contract had never been completed. From my perspective, she kept changing her mind. What should have been a thirty-day project ended up taking over a year and a half. We never formally decided to part ways but instead just let time pass. I've learned the hard way that things neglected over time only get worse. We build up stories about others; judgment and blame grow. After seeing this client at the conference, I knew I had to send one more email.

It went something like this:

> Hey there,
> I wanted to reach out to you to ask for your forgiveness.
> In the conclusion of our working together last year, I have come to realize that I could have handled the transition better than I did.
> Words I said, the quality of work delivered, and my general attitude did not reflect my better self.
> I apologize for any harm I have caused you.
> Will you forgive me?
>
> Brian

As with the thirty-plus emails before, I thought I would receive a "No problem, thanks for being so cool" email in response. Instead she snapped back a few minutes later.

> If your desire is to make it right, then I think I deserve a refund.

Ouch.

I did not like where this conversation was going. We were just a few weeks away from Christmas and the end of the calendar year, one of the busiest seasons for my business. Dreading the potentially negative response, I took a deep breath and wrote her back.

> That's fair. What do you think would make it right?

Since I was at my home office, I walked downstairs to tell my wife, Julie, that something big was coming. "Hey, honey." She was decorating pine cone ornaments with our two youngest kids. "I really feel like I might have to send a refund to an old coaching client. Are you cool with that?" Julie and I have learned that sometimes the hardest thing to do is the right thing to do. "Yep," she replied knowingly. "If that's what we need to do." I walked back up to my office to await the reply. A few minutes later, after I refreshed my email a dozen times, there it was in black and white.

> I appreciate your integrity in this and think splitting it at $750 would be fair.

I logged in to PayPal and immediately sent the money. I forwarded my old client the receipt and said I hoped this would help us move forward. And I thanked her for giving me the opportunity to make things right.

The email I received in reply is worth framing. Whenever I'm feeling down, whenever I'm discouraged by a client or a business challenge, I look for that old email still archived in my inbox. It reads,

> Thanks, Brian—I'm having trouble coming up with the words to express what I want to say, but I know you didn't need to reach out at all *or* agree to a refund, and both speak volumes to your character. I'm glad to know you!

Wow. With only a small gesture, I had turned an adversary into an advocate.

By considering her perspective and taking responsibility for my actions and their consequences, intended or not, I was set free. And there is freedom for you too.

I recently saw this client again at a conference where I shared this story from the stage. She's referred clients to me, asked for my advice, and told me how much she has seen me change.

There is hope for you, my friend. Here's what I've come to believe as a result of all this deep relationship work: Every day, we have a choice. We make a decision whether to start with our people each and every day. We can choose to have a people-first mindset or a project-first mindset.

When we choose to put people last, we make decisions that we'll one day regret. We choose the hurry of a busy day. We ignore a simple request until it snowballs into an avalanche of awkwardness. We forget to express gratitude to our team or our family, and a seed is planted. A weed of discontent takes root and grows until it chokes the life from our most important relationships.

But it does not have to be that way. You can choose to start with your people, to show up each day seeing and serving the people in your life. Change starts when you shift your focus outward to serving others. Deciding to put people first isn't easy. It often requires doing something we don't want to do.

When we start with people, we have clarity of purpose, a plan for our daily practice, and a path to profit. We experience a new level of freedom in our lives and in our work. We live authentically, serving those around us with joy and deference.

Starting with people changes the way we work; we recognize the people we do the work for.

Starting with people changes the way we lead; we connect with the people on our team.

Starting with people changes the way we relate; we see the needs of those around us.

As a business and career coach, I am often asked by clients,

"How do I figure out my purpose?" My answer is surprisingly blunt. "You already know your purpose. Just look around at the people in your life. See where they're stuck? Help them get unstuck. Start with your people. People are your purpose."

Now that you know the who and before I show you the how, I need to confess something to you. I am the last person who should be writing this book, because I don't naturally love people. In my darkest depths, there is a man who sees people as a means to an end, vehicles for getting me closer to what I want. Others are often an afterthought.

As you can imagine, this has caused me more pain and trouble than I care to admit; it is my greatest shame and my most embarrassing weakness. It has impacted my friendships, my clients, and my family.

In my perfect, self-first world, I do my job, others do theirs, we dutifully play our roles, and everyone gets along just fine. You do what you need to do to get ahead, and if you miss out on an opportunity, well, too bad. That's on you. Learn the rules of the game if you want to be a skilled player.

The problem is that when things inevitably go awry, I allow my inner judge to emerge. I put on my black robe, bang my gavel, and demand order in the court. But life is not a courtroom, and I am not the judge of everyone.

I never set out to be manipulative or conniving, but over the years, because of my driven, me-first approach, I burned a lot of bridges. I created a trail of fragmented and broken relationships and a long line of people who thought poorly of me, and I don't blame them. When projects failed, I came up with arrogant excuses to justify my shortcomings and point in their direction. "This result has nothing to do with me," I proclaimed. "You just can't handle the heat. You don't have the same level of commitment to success."

But the last few years have been different. After my 360 Assessment, I began to see people again. I've learned to take full responsibility. I've seen the value of building relationships instead of tearing them down. I've recognized when relationships need a quick check-in, a short apology, or a small gesture toward unity. And it has made a dramatic difference.

My relationships are stronger, my business has grown, and there are more opportunities than ever before.

When you make the daily decision to start with your people, things will change for you too. Yes, there will be bumps along the road, but the journey is worth it. This book will serve as your map. So join me in the pursuit of living a people-first lifestyle. It will open up opportunities and give you more clarity than you've ever experienced.

Remember, you get to choose. Each day, you decide your priority. I challenge you to put people first. It's the daily decision that changes everything.

Ideas to Consider

- Growing in work and in our lives often requires taking a hard, honest look at ourselves.
- A 360 Assessment helps us gain honest feedback from current and past associates.
- Receiving positive feedback is fun, but it is the negative feedback that provides the most insight.
- It will require courage to reach out to those providing feedback, in order to gain the most benefit.
- Facing the difficult things about ourselves helps us know where we can grow.

Actions to Take

- Ask yourself each morning and throughout the day, "What can I do to treat people like they matter?"
- Ask people you have worked with in the past to evaluate you through a 360 Assessment. What positive things did you learn about yourself? What areas challenged you and made you face something difficult about yourself?
- Consider where focusing on your people would make the biggest impact in your life and work. Identify three areas and list action steps you would like to take to shift, change, or add to your current practice.

CHAPTER 2

The Power of a Simple
Daily Decision

Every morning, you make a decision. You choose what comes first.

It's an attitude that proceeds the action. It's the sail you set in the direction you want to go. And every day, you get to choose where you start.

Most start with practice. A daily routine. Get up, get going, get it done.

Others start with profit. The daily grind. Work is a necessary slog to put food on the table.

A few look to purpose, waking up with joy to do work that matters.

But I believe there is a better way to begin your day. Start with your people.

There are two steps. See and serve. Notice the people in your life. Look at them. See them. Observe where they are stuck and ask, "What do they need from me today? How can I help?" And then serve. Take action. Offer your assistance. Show that you care. That's it.

Starting with your people means intentionally seeing and serving those already in your life. It means reorienting your life so that instead of starting with your concerns, you become a student of theirs. Your family. Your team. Your friends and neighbors. Start with them. It's the daily decision that changes everything.

Imagine what your life would be like if you were to start with your people. If you began with their needs and desires—not with your purpose or profits but with what your people need and want from you and the work you do.

I used to think that as long as I delivered the results people were after, everyone would be happy.

But it doesn't work that way.

When we focus on goals and forget about people, achievement rings hollow. We can hit our goals but completely miss our people.

- You can get that big promotion at work but come home to a marriage in shambles.
- You can be the go-to leader in your industry but step over people to get there.
- You can sell everyone on your great idea but struggle to connect with a team to help you.

People matter. A life of profitable purpose starts with focusing on your people—listening to them, showing up for them, and serving them. This is the key to building the skills it takes to grow and unlocking the door to opportunity and work that matters. You can make an impact and an income through reputation, results, and referrals.

You don't need to know the whole path. You just need to be faithful with what is in front of you.

This is the people-first way to live.

And starting with them takes just a few small actions every day. From sending a text message when you're running late instead of blaming traffic, to asking a friend if they need anything while you're still at the store, to sending an email to clear the air about that big project instead of waiting until Monday, putting people first is a daily decision.

It may be simple, but it isn't easy. When something challenges us, it also has the power to change us.

The lives we lead, the projects we manage, the work we do—all add up, and the only measure that really matters is the way we treat the people in our lives. How we treat them, how we help them, how we truly see them can change everything.

Imagine seeing the people in your life as advocates instead of adversaries.

Starting with your people can turn a hard-driving entrepreneur like me into a heart-centered coach. It can save marriages, heal broken friendships, and end workplace rivalries. It can help us love our work again. And we can wake up with purpose and passion, ready to fight off the voices nudging us toward mediocrity. So let's begin this journey together.

Ideas to Consider

- We can hit our goals but completely miss our people.
- Every day, we can choose whether we put people first.
- The work you do can make an impact on the people you care about.
- Success and achievements don't mean much if there is no one to celebrate them with.
- Achievements in the workplace should not come at the expense of our relationships.
- We can enjoy success in our work and in our relationships simultaneously.

Actions to Take

- Make a list of the people who are important to you.
- Access a list of ideas of how you can serve them at startwithyourpeople.com/ideas.
- Decide on one specific action you can take to help someone in the next 24 hours. Then post the results at startwithyourpeople.com/action.

PART 1

PEOPLE

Seeing Those Already in Our Lives

It was too hot to be wearing a suit.

A friend had recently lost his mom, and we were here to celebrate her life and say goodbye. Honestly, the timing was terrible. I was in the middle of yet another online product launch, and it was all hands on deck. The cell phone reception was awful. Yet this funeral was more important.

As we walked to the front door of the funeral home, it hit me, as if for the first time: these are my people. My young son holding my hand, about to experience his first funeral. My aging mom and dad. My sister and brother-in-law. My dear wife, Julie. My client making the cell phone in my pocket vibrate. And my team handling launch day issues while I went offline for a few hours.

I had never met Marie. I'd heard stories and seen pictures, but there was no personal connection, which allowed me to be more of an observer. I was used to being onstage, serving as the speaker or teacher. But this was different. I had no role to perform. No part to play. I was free to just take it all in.

As the service progressed, through stories, songs, and prayers, I clearly saw the culmination of a life. No one mentioned her worldly possessions or what she was leaving behind. Instead everyone remembered the difference she made for people.

Attending Marie's funeral let me see how our lives impact others and how tiny actions add up to a narrative arc of a life well lived. I couldn't help but consider that one day stories would be told about me.

We spend so much time living our lives yet so little time designing our legacy. When our life is over, there's very little that will live on after us. When we really get down to it, our main legacy will be the investment we made in people.

I'm willing to make a bet that the most beloved, admired legacies are those of ordinary men and women who made the daily choice to start with their people. And that's a choice we get to make too.

But let's face it. There is more to life than what is said at our funeral.

People can be complicated. At first, entering into a relationship is invigorating. We anticipate things working out. A new business, relationship, or job opportunity. We start to count the results before we've taken any action. It's all so exciting.

And then somewhere along the way, reality sets in. The results come in, and there is this feeling that it worked or it failed. People can get in our way, ruin our day, and then misunderstandings abound, something happens, and we snap to judgment. In the heat of the moment, words are said, promises are undone, and criticisms are launched. Ending a relationship after things don't work out is exhausting.

Crafting a legacy is a daily refining of our rough edges, a series of intentional actions taken every day. And often, it's not easy.

Working with people requires thick skin, a strong stomach, and a soft heart. We all bring a set of expectations to the table.

Deep down, we know how we want to be treated. Unfair treatment can be frustrating to observe, but often it can help us clarify our values.

- A boss mistreating her employees bolsters our resolve: "I will respect every member of my team."
- A dad berating his son in a parking lot reminds you, "I will guard my child's heart, no matter how angry I am."
- A relative's harsh words to her spouse convict you, "We will never talk to each other like that."

Use that frustration to fuel you. Let the negative examples you see reinforce the positive person you want to be. Let them lead you to living a people-first life.

It's easy to think that nobody really notices the choices you're making except for the people closest to you. Over time, I've learned that our reputation precedes us. This means that every action you take will affect other people personally and professionally. You let someone park ahead of you and find another spot. You donate when a charity calls or knocks on your door. You volunteer for social programs to help those in need. The actions of your life create a ripple effect, a wave of care for others. When we are doing work that we love, serving people well, and living in our sweet spot, we find the joy of life.

But living and working with people on a daily basis is not easy. There are times when our values differ, our opinions conflict, our viewpoints diverge. And these struggles can take their toll.

Tyler, an attorney, was in the trenches every day, fighting for his clients and being attacked by other attorneys. Eventually, the burden was just too heavy to bear. He found himself divorced and in a rehabilitation facility. It was all just too much to take.

Megan, a dental assistant, was miserable. She realized her boss was pressuring patients into services they didn't need instead of truly serving them. She wanted to quit, but her family needed the money.

And then there's Dave, a bestselling author, making more money than he ever thought possible, yet he wasn't happier for it. The last time I saw him, there was no life left in his eyes. He was still on the hunt, chasing the next high, launching yet another book, hoping to hit the *New York Times* bestseller list again, and he was simply exhausted. Years of relentless grit and hustle finally drove him to the breaking point. A deep depression, a far-off look in his eyes, and uncharacteristic critical comments.

But what if things were different? What if each of these friends of mine were fully engaged with the people in their life?

Engagement. It's been a key word in my life for more than twenty years. As a classroom teacher and school administrator, I noticed that engagement was the key distinction between teachers who made a difference in their students' lives and teachers who just showed up for a paycheck. Engagement was the difference between a school that felt alive, focused on student achievement, and a school that just felt hopeless.

I've seen it in the workplace too. Disengaged workers waiting for the weekend, waiting for the end of their shift, waiting for things to change. But for things to change, first you need to change. Engagement is a choice. Engagement means showing up and serving your people. And full engagement brings light to even the darkest of circumstances.

I know this, because I've experienced what it means to be fully engaged. When we are engaged in our work, our calling, and our daily tasks, we are, as my friend and inspirational speaker Kary Oberbrunner says, "a soul on fire."

You want to fulfill your profitable purpose, but you may not love your job right now. You're counting down the days until your next vacation. You check the time until you can finally go home. You stare at the clock until the meeting ends. You're checked out, disengaged, and just coasting through life. Is that how you want to live?

Maybe you're a business leader and you're frustrated with your team's lack of engagement. They haven't bought into the vision, and there's no way they'll strive to make your company a people-first brand. You hear about other organizations winning Best Place to Work awards and talking about their staff like they're family, and you shake your head, believing it isn't possible for you. I know, I've been there.

Perhaps you're working independently. You started your side hustle, or you're a full-time entrepreneur. You might be a mom trying to grow her business at night while managing a hectic life by day, or you might be trying to nurture a business from scratch. You focus on generating an income and putting best practices into place, but you're not communicating your purpose in a way that appeals to new customers and clients. Sales is just a word, and marketing is something you would rather ignore. There's got to be a better way.

Regardless of how you categorize your life season, business, or style, you're a leader. Your family, your team, and your clients need you to lead with them in mind.

Are you

- Stuck?
- Loathing your current job?
- Struggling to maintain balance between work and home?
- Pulled in opposite directions as you try to engage with your spouse and kids?
- Desperate to show up and do a good job?
- Having trouble getting hired?
- Being passed over for that promotion?
- Dealing with constant interruptions?
- Unable to find the right clients?

The solution is simple.

Start with your people.

Don't start with your passion, your why, your talents, or your experience. Start with the people you will impact.

People lead to purpose.

Purpose leads to profit.

Profit leads to practice.

I think back to Marie's funeral. The life she lived, the people she impacted, and the legacy she left. One day, your people will gather to honor your life. To say goodbye and to recount the memories of the times you shared with them. What do you want them to say? How do you want to be remembered? Your actions in the present will influence their words in the future.

Imagine having clarity of purpose, because you know who you are, why you're here, and how you can serve others.

Imagine being known as a top performer, generating more income than you ever thought possible, and serving your dream customer—starting where you already are.

Picture your life with the right rhythms and routines to maximize rest, reflection, and meaningful work. It's all possible when you start with your people.

Ideas to Consider

Engaging with your people is key to living a fulfilling, purposeful life.

- Your people include everyone you interact with, not just your family, friends, and coworkers.
- Let the negative examples you see reinforce the positive person you want to be.
- Your lasting legacy will be reflected in your level of engagement with those around you.

Work

The Best Place to Start

with Your People

We choose how we treat our coworkers and customers. We decide the level of energy, effort, and attention we give our customers, colleagues, and superiors.

I recently asked my followers on Facebook, "When it comes to a 'job' (past or present), what are your biggest annoyances?"

Here are just a few of the issues they brought up.

> People that don't pull their own weight and expect you to cover for them or do the actual work for them.
>
> —David

> Bosses who don't make their expectations clear or have trouble handing over work.
>
> —Gretchen

> Toxic atmospheres where respect is nonexistent.
>
> —Leah

Work can be frustrating, overwhelming, and discouraging. It's no wonder 87 percent of today's workforce is disengaged.

But it doesn't have to be that way.

You don't have to quit your job to find the joy in your work.

Instead what would it be like if you were fully engaged in your daily work? Even if you don't love your job right now, what if you changed your perspective, attitude, and effort to do the best job possible? To change your work environment, it's time to put people first. More than twenty years ago, in his book *The Human Equation: Building Profits by Putting People First*, Stanford University professor Jeffrey Pfeffer explained, "Companies that put people first consistently outperform those that don't."[1]

And it's still true today.

In this first section of the book, we're going to focus on the people we work with: our clients, our team, and our boss.

---

1   Jeffrey Pfeffer, *The Human Equation: Building Profits by Putting People First* (Boston: Harvard Business School Press, 1998), 74.

CHAPTER 3

Clients

Everything You Want Begins by

Serving Your Ideal Client

---

wanted to give up. The business I'd started just a few years before wasn't growing. I had a consulting project here and a coaching client there but nothing sustainable and no real clarity about where I was headed. I was frustrated and discouraged. I did my best to hold it inside, to fake it until I made it, to play the part of the successful business owner when in reality things were not going as I had planned. And then one day, I got a call from my pastor. He told me about Jack.

Jack was in his midfifties, had recently lost his job, and was thinking about starting a blog. As a favor, my pastor asked me to meet with Jack over lunch. He said, "Maybe you could give Jack a little encouragement and direction." I specifically remember him saying "encouragement and direction." I thought, *That's what I need.* So I put it on my calendar. A few days later there I was, in a coffee shop, sitting across the table from Jack. And boy, did he need some encouragement and direction! I started coaching, helping him clarify his vision for his new website.

I helped Jack pick his domain name, built his website, and worked with him over several sessions to get his first few posts written. Admittedly, it wasn't my dream project, but I showed up and did the work. At our last meeting over coffee, I presented Jack with the final version of his blog. He was overjoyed. He loved the site and was so pleased with the results. I was happy to help him but didn't see how this small project could lead anywhere for me and my business. And then, over my shoulder, I heard a voice. "Do you work on blogs?"

Jack jumped right in. "Yes!" he said. "He just finished mine. He's really good!" Katie, a beginning speaker, hired me on the spot to create a blog for her. I came home from the coffee shop encouraged from landing a new client. I couldn't see the path, but at least I knew the next right step.

I met with Katie a few times, and we worked together to get her blog off the ground. As I was leaving our final meeting, she told me about an upcoming bloggers conference she was attending a few hours away. I reached out to the conference planner and offered my services. My email said, "I help authors and speakers take their online message to the next level by helping with their strategy and their website."

Up until that point, I had helped only Jack and Katie. I felt like a bit of an imposter writing that email. A few days later, I heard back from the conference planner, who offered me the option to pay to sponsor the conference. We didn't have the money, but I did have time and hustle. I offered to get on the phone with her and figure something out.

During that call, I listened to her vision for the conference. I asked her what the conference attendees struggled with the most.

She had a clear answer. "Honestly, most of them have a really tough time with their websites." I offered to set up a booth at the conference and answer website questions. She agreed, and I knew that this was an opportunity to meet potential clients.

I created an online link where conference attendees could book fifteen-minute website consultation appointments. I thought I might help ten or fifteen people.

In the opening session of the conference, the emcee announced the link to sign up for website consultation appointments. Within a matter of minutes, all seventy-four fifteen-minute appointments were filled. That represented eighteen and a half hours of free consultation. Over two exhausting, exhilarating days, I learned exactly where my ideal clients were stuck. For the first time, I realized that what is obvious to me is magic to other people.

That's the foundation of your business. You are a professional problem solver. Your clients need you to solve their problems. That's how you start with your people at work: by identifying and fixing their problems. That's what it means to run a people-first business.

I'd love to tell you that things magically became clear in my work from that point forward. But many times, it would have been easier to give up. And just when I felt like giving up, I would turn to my growing list of email subscribers and ask, "Where are you stuck right now?" Each time, I'd get the clarity I needed to create the next product or training program. Over time, business started to come to me.

Your Work Is for Their Dreams

Of all the jobs I've had, from flipping burgers to teaching in a classroom to running a coaching business, one factor has remained constant. Whatever I was doing, success wasn't just about doing the job. It was about serving the people through my job.

No matter what your job is, at the end of the day, you are there to help people accomplish their dreams. Their dream may be to run to the grocery store to find what they want at a reasonable price. Their dream may be to have a successful birthday party for a five-year-old, and they need balloons from you—now. Their dream may be to get home from a long trip, and they need you to help them get there as quickly as possible.

When you see your job as helping people accomplish their dreams, even though you have the same job, your job has changed. You are in the people-serving business, because you are a professional problem solver. And here's the surprising truth. It is a lot of fun! It's invigorating to help real people solve meaningful problems. You don't have to quit your job to love your life. You can love what you do right now, at the stage of life you are in right now.

Everything you do is to help other people accomplish their dreams.

Dream Clients

We all know what it's like to be treated second best. It's offensive. It's off-putting. When someone chooses their lunch break or company policy over serving a customer, it causes frustration and anger. We all know how we expect to be treated. We know how to give people special favors and extra service and make them feel valued. If our grandmother were visiting our restaurant, dental office, or workplace, we would give her the preferred-customer treatment. This is what our customers want. This is what our team members want.

You can be part of the solution to their problem by authentically serving them and having a blast doing work you love. Seeing your work through the lens of service changes everything.

Peter, a coaching client of mine, was a career coach and corporate consultant who really struggled in his business. He was trying to serve everybody. He was hesitant to choose a niche because he felt like he was going to leave potential clients behind.

During one of our online video coaching calls, I asked him to dream with me for a minute. "Imagine you have an afternoon free at a bookstore. No kids. No responsibilities. Just the freedom to browse. Where do you go?" He answered right away: outdoor life, adventure sports, and anything to do with mountain climbing.

I said, "Imagine if you could take the services you provide, helping people get clear on their career and grow their business, but you focus only on that adventure sports niche." Peter's eyes lit up. "Imagine," I continued, "if you became the best-known career coach in the adventure sports industry. What would that mean for your business? Would it shrink or would it grow?"

The answer was obvious. Peter's whole demeanor changed because for the first time, he could clearly see the opportunity right in front of him.

We talked about developing an intake process to nurture and recruit his ideal clients. Suddenly his work with teachers in a small church preschool no longer fit his vivid vision.

Over the course of the next few coaching calls, I helped him clarify and refine his branding and online sales process. Peter learned that positioning your company for success is all about being authentic. Your dream client wants to know you are the perfect match for their needs because you get them. They are part of your tribe.

Instead of Peter having to shave his beard and trade in his plaid flannel shirt for a dress shirt and tie, he is able to be himself. His uniqueness is his strategic advantage.

A specific vision leads to greater abundance. People do business with people they know, like, and trust. Narrow your target to widen your reach. I know it seems counterintuitive. But it's absolutely true.

If people do business with those they know, like, and trust, how do you help make sure they know, like, and trust you? People get to know you during your interactions in the sales process, through talking and listening. People like you because they see themselves in you as you make a connection with them. They trust you because you have shown them the results you've gotten for others and helped them see how they can experience these same results for themselves. They believe that you can help them accomplish their dreams.

Whether you're a customer service representative, an entrepreneur, or the head of the company, you are in sales. Sales is not about the product. It's about providing a solution for a person. Start with the person on the other side of the screen or the other end of the phone. Who are they? What are their needs? What are their hopes? When you know this, you can turn to your products and hand them the right fit. The great motivational speaker Zig Ziglar often said, "You can have everything in life you want if you will just help enough other people get what they want."[1] Zig started with his people.

For fourteen years, I worked in K–12 education, first as a classroom teacher and later as the founder of a charter school. Being a classroom teacher was often a thankless job. Teachers juggle multiple demands: classroom management, kids from different backgrounds with diverse skills and abilities, administration, parents—all kinds of issues. But successful teachers start with the students in their classroom. Who are they? What are they good at? Where are they struggling? What are their needs? What have they already gone through?

All of these questions are focused on who. Successful teachers meet kids where they are and help them get to where they're going. They start with their people.

In my first year of teaching, I learned a secret from a veteran teacher, Miss D. She taught an after-school program that she viewed

---

1   Zig Ziglar, *Secrets of Closing the Sale* (Grand Rapids: Revell, 1984), 42.

as a tool to recruit her ideal students and families. That's right. She was a public school teacher, with a roster of students from the public school system, in which she had no say or control. Yet she still saw her role as being in the recruitment process.

Everywhere she went, she talked about the good work we were doing at our school. Over time, students from other schools and other grades began attending her summer camp and her after-school program. Over the course of the year, I heard stories of families who moved into the school's district in order to be taught by Miss D. She was proof that people take an interest in you when you take an interest in them.

Make it your mission to make their day.

Imagine that your ninety-two-year-old grandmother is a new client at your company. What would you do to roll out the red carpet for her? What would you do to give her the best possible service? Make a list with your team of what it would take to go above and beyond for your grandmother. After completing it, look at your team and ask, "Why can't we do this every day in our company?"

What if you sought to make this your mission each day?

The waitress assumes she is just serving another table and tries to hurry the customers along. Little does she know that a son is meeting his birth mom for the first time.

The gas station attendant thinks he is just pumping gas but doesn't know he is helping a nervous, first-time dad make sure the vehicle has enough gas to get to the hospital in time for the birth of his new baby.

The fitness instructor believes she is just leading her Wednesday morning class but doesn't know the self-doubt her new student had to fight just to walk into the gym for the first time.

These stories are happening all around us.

If we take the opportunity to make their day, to help put a smile on their face, imagine what our world would be like. What if we treated every order, every interaction, like it was a life-altering event? Because often it is.

It's not easy.

The customers you work with, the clients you serve, the people who frequent your company might be challenging. They might not feel like "your people." It might be hard to see them with empathy and relate to them personally.

You might wish you could work somewhere else. I get it.

But the solution is to work with them instead of around them. The key is finding ways to serve them.

Those people who come into your office or frequent your business location are your customers. That's who you have right now, and you are tasked with serving them well. Do well for the people who are already in your life.

I've consulted with companies and organizations that are struggling to grow. I've even heard a twinge of resentment from clients, wishing their customers and guests were different. Instead of serving the people they have now, they are dissatisfied with their current customers, wishing to work with someone else. But resentment is not the solution.

What if you could turn it around and see your current customers as your dream customers? What if you treated them like VIPs? For things to be different, you need to make the difference. When you go to work tomorrow, see the people who are there as if for the first time. Treat them like the incredible people they are, even if you haven't seen that side of them yet.

Instead of being annoyed, be thankful for the people who ask you the dumb questions, who walk into your business confused or call the office overwhelmed. They need you to bring your best and to show up for them. You are the solution to the problem they have. And you decide how you respond to them. That's what a people-first leader does. She sees the person behind the problem and offers her assistance. It's the way we want to be treated, and treating others with respect and dignity goes a long way. Everything changes when we start with our people.

Ideas to Consider

- What may be obvious to you is magic to someone else.
- Instead of thinking about what you do, see your work through the lens of who you serve.
- Sales is not about the product; it's about providing a solution for a person.
- Following the thread of our successes gives us a good idea of who our ideal clients are.
- When we understand that our job is helping our clients achieve their dreams, the choices we make in our business are designed to accomplish that goal.
- When the transformation of our clients matters deeply to us, our business begins to take on more meaning and grows organically as we become better problem solvers for our people.

Actions to Take

- Listen to your customers to see where they need direction and encouragement.
- Brainstorm a list of what you know that may not be obvious to someone else.
- Consider what would make a really cool experience for your customers.

CHAPTER 4

Team

You've Already Found

Your Dream Team

The best word to describe it is awkward. We were minutes away from the beginning of the first of many open house nights for the brand-new charter school I was working so hard to launch. And what had been months of work to get ready was all going to pay off tonight. I was uncomfortable in my suit and tie. We were in an unfamiliar environment, a fancy art gallery space, waiting for the arrival of people we'd never met. We didn't have any students. We didn't have a building. We didn't have any teachers. But we did have a team.

It was a small team—just five of us—but we believed that over time, things would grow. And I remember looking around at the small group of people and thinking, *This is my team. And we're here for one reason: our students.*

Over the next several months, we hosted dozens of these open houses. But it's that first one that stays in my memory, because before we had any clients or any other stakeholders, I had a team. They were my dream team.

Sure, each one of us had faults. But together we delivered results, because we shared the same mission.

Our goal was to impact kids by opening an innovative high school that would help students whom the public school system had all but given up on get to college and pursue a brighter future. None of these first five team members were the teachers or administrators who would work with the kids. Their job was focused on the logistics of getting the school open. But because of their hard work and dedication and our focused mission, we overcame innumerable obstacles and opened the school with more than two hundred students in less than six months.

The next few years were really hard. We had trouble hiring the right teachers, and we had trouble keeping the great ones. There are all kinds of issues and challenges in getting a school started. But maintaining the vision and staying on the same page as a team was the toughest! Most of the mistakes we made along the way were because of a lack of unity.

After three years on the job—leading this growing organization, serving more than five hundred students and more than thirty teachers and staff members—I hosted a leadership getaway at a retreat center about an hour and a half out of town. Our team had been through a lot, but as we were playing a game of charades, laughing and connecting, I remember thinking, *This is my dream team*. And here's my realization. It's all about your mindset. Your team will never be perfect. But they are your team!

I want you to think about your work and the people you work with every day. Your boss, your coworkers, everybody involved in your life at work. That is your dream team. Do you see it? Can you picture it? I know, you might have to squint a little in order to really see it. You might have that one coworker who just doesn't belong. That one team member who is always on your back, telling you what you're doing wrong. Or that one employee who just doesn't pull his weight.

But imagine if the team you currently work with were actually your dream team. What would it mean for your clients to be able to engage with that dream team? What would it mean for your enthusiasm about going to work each day if you were able to work with the best people in your industry? How much fun would it be to do work you love with a team you love? This is what is possible when you decide to be a people-first leader.

I'll admit it here. I haven't done a very good job at this in the past. I've looked at a coworker and wished he would just retire. I've been in situations in which I couldn't wait for a boss to go on maternity leave so I could finally get my work done. I've avoided working on projects with a fellow employee because I couldn't stand his personality. I'm sure you can relate.

Somewhere along the way, there was a misunderstanding. Something happened. Somebody dropped the ball, somebody was late, somebody didn't quite tell the whole truth. A crack formed, and over time it divided the team. People started to pick sides. They retreated to their corners and held on to their positions. And unity was lost. The common bond we all had—being on the same mission for our clients and customers—was pushed aside for our own purposes and priorities. And everyone suffered. Work was no longer fun. The drudgery set in and compromise began. One coworker was late to a meeting. Another turned in their report late. Another gossiped about someone else. And dissension rose among the ranks. And now we're left to deal with the mess. Disorganization, chaos, and infighting are the new normal. We've gotten so used to it that it doesn't even hurt anymore.

But what if things could be different? What if you were to see the team you have as the team you dream about? What if you were to give them a chance? What would change for you?

No more evenings complaining about that one team member. No more wasted weekends grumbling about how you're dreading Monday. No more scanning job websites, hoping for a transition to get you out of that mess.

Get to Know Them

One thing I've learned is that the more you get to know someone, the more you discover about them. You learn the reasons why they are the way they are. When you hear their stories, you develop more empathy for their plight in life. And although it might not excuse their bad behavior, you begin to develop an understanding.

For us to start with our people at work, we need to get to know them. We need to learn what their motivation is. What gets them up in the morning? What's important to them? Knowing these things will show you another side of your team. And you might just discover something hidden in plain sight. You might just see that you're already working with your dream team.

What if you made it your goal to help your team win? Instead of trying to hold them accountable or catch them doing something wrong, what if you made it your personal goal to help them succeed? How would things change for you and for your company?

Dealing with a Difficult Team Member

I've dedicated an entire chapter to strategies for dealing with difficult people, because we meet difficult people in every area of our life. But while you're here, I'll just share one tip for dealing with a difficult person at work: make it your mission to win that person over. Often, it's hearing them out, connecting with them, asking for a favor, or showing that you need them. Tiny gestures can go a long way.

Getting to Know Your Team

I believe that every person on your team is there for a reason. She got the job; she's working in the industry for a specific purpose. Now, she may have long forgotten that purpose, but there's a reason she started. When you know why she does what she does, you can work with her in a way that brings her life, energy, and confidence and serves you because of the relationship and trust you've built with her. We notice the weaknesses and assume the strengths; instead we need to notice the strengths and name them.

Your team member might seem like an insufferable, miserable person, but someone in their life loves them. It might be their mom or their spouse, but somebody sees the good in them. Can you do the same?

Winning Them Over

Back in college, there was a girl in my major with whom I had three classes one semester, and it was difficult to get along with her. Because of our shared class schedule, I knew I would be seeing a lot of her, and I was not looking forward to it. Early in the semester, I came across the old English proverb "It's easier to catch flies with honey than with vinegar." It was then that I realized my negative attitude about her was not helping anyone. It was only hurting me.

So I decided to make her day. I'd overheard that she liked tulips, so I ordered some tulips and put them in her campus mailbox with an anonymous typed note that just said, "I hope you have a great day."

That little gesture did two things. First, she was very positive for that day, so that was a short-term win. But the second, long-term win was that I had a secret. I had helped her. Once I got the positive feeling of having encouraged her, I wanted to do it more. And I kind of hate to admit it, but she got less annoying. I also realized that I started treating her differently. And before too long, she reciprocated my kindness. She recommended me for a leadership position. We served on a committee together. And when we graduated college the next year, I could genuinely say that we had become friends. And it all started with an anonymous bouquet of flowers.

So here is the application. If somebody at work is driving you crazy, find a way to make their day. What can you do to defuse the grudge they may have against you? As leadership guru Stephen Covey wrote, "We judge ourselves by our intentions and others by their behavior."[1] You may have the best of intentions, but your actions have not shown your best character. Your team is judging you according to what you've done and how you've treated them, the looks you've given and the words you've said. Changing the relationship starts with changing your behavior toward them.

Clarify Expectations

One of the keys to working well with your team is having clear expectations. Clarifying expectations will help to alleviate much of the tension you experience. I have found that the majority of issues I experience in business, at our church, in friendship groups,

---

1   Stephen M. R. Covey, *The Speed of Trust: The One Thing That Changes Everything* (New York: Simon and Schuster, 2006), 13.

on committees I serve on, and definitely in family situations come down to expectations.

Expectations are promises we make to ourselves on behalf of someone else. The challenge is often that the person is unaware that we have claimed that territory for them. They have no clue that we're expecting them to engage at that particular level. Yes, they might recall a conversation or an idea, but unless it was written down and signed, it's really hard to pin someone down to say specifically that your expectation was on track.

This isn't something I've perfected, but what I've learned is to clarify expectations, to the point that it's almost impossible for somebody to miss the commitment that they're making. Ideally, it's written down and signed. Most times—particularly after a meeting—when people talk about the different roles, I'll type up the expectations. This is the goal of the project. Here's your job, with bullet points. Here's my job, with bullet points. Go into as much detail as possible. Make it a regular practice to clarify expectations with your team members.

Let Them Go with Grace

When someone leaves your team, your church, your email list, your whatever, wish them well. Cheer for their success. In many industries I consult in, one of the largest challenges that leaders face is employee turnover. The team you have is likely to change frequently. People are constantly changing jobs or needing to be let go. If we start with our people, then we let them go with grace. Whether they decide to quit or you need to fire them, what can you do to let them go with grace? How can you help them maintain their dignity in the process?

I once had an incredible intern. I would have loved to work with her forever. I coached her, mentored her, and encouraged her, and she ended up resigning, getting another job, and pursuing other opportunities. Here's the thing: she has referred clients to me time and time again. I look back on our time together and say, "I'm really glad I invested in her." That's how you should treat your team. Treat your team like you want to be treated. You can't hold on to your team forever. Be excited for their success, even if that means they leave you.

One of the first years of our school, we had a teacher who was becoming increasingly frustrated. Issues at home were beginning to leak into her work. And she had come to resent the work she was doing. It got back to me from students that she was planning on quitting and making a big scene. After confirming that this was true, I knew I had to let her go immediately.

Instead of bringing her into my office and lambasting her, telling her all the horrible things that she was doing, I invited her out for coffee. We walked to a nearby coffee shop, and I asked her about her dreams. "What got you into education in the first place? What is it you love about being a teacher?" And we had an amazing conversation.

For more than an hour, I got to listen to what she really wanted out of life. And honestly, so much of my impression of her changed during that conversation. But I still had to let her go.

Over our second cup of cappuccino, I said, "I do have some bad news. Unfortunately, this needs to be your last day."

I expected her to lash out. Or maybe to burst into tears. Or worse, to finally say all of the words she had been holding in.

Instead her response was calm and measured. "I know."

We walked back to the school, sharing funny stories about our students. There was no bitterness. No fear. Just acknowledgment.

Even having to fire someone can be done with a people-first mindset. I'm the first to admit that I don't always get this right. I've failed in this area more times than I'd like to remember.

But here's what I know to be true. When we treat people with dignity and let them go with grace, even if they decide to leave on their own, the conversation changes.

As a team member and as a leader, I challenge you to be *for* people. Be on their side. Stand with them even if they are leaving. Let them know that you are cheering for their success. It costs you nothing, but it means everything.

Ideas to Consider

- It takes intention and nurturing to turn a disgruntled team member into a real asset.
- Seeing team members as real people with real needs helps us develop a better dream team for our company, project, or organization.
- When we see team members as people with lives and needs beyond their job descriptions, we have a better perspective of how to nurture each one toward greatness and bring them into the mission of the team.

Actions to Take

- Set clear expectations and communicate these in friendly but clearly written forms.
- Take meeting notes and send out a follow-up email to indicate what's expected of each person.
- Plan meetings and off-site get-togethers to connect with your team members on a more personal and caring level.
- Think of a leader who helped you develop as a person. Write out some of your most vivid memories. How did these contribute to your success long after you moved on to another team?

■ List your dream team members. How do you envision your dream team working together? Next, list the strengths of each member. Reflect on how to maximize these strengths to match your vision and mission. What one thing can you do today to start making that happen?

CHAPTER 5

Boss

Your Number One Client

No matter what industry you are in, you have only one client and one job. Your client is your boss. And your job is to make your boss look awesome. Your job is not just to do your job. When you help your boss accomplish his or her goals, it always helps you as well. But many of my clients through the years have told me they have a tenuous relationship with their boss. Maybe you work with an absentee boss or one who is not particularly inspirational, or perhaps one who is unfair. But here is the truth, my friends: your boss is the gatekeeper to your career goals. It's up to you to win your boss over. I believe your life will be better if you do well by your boss. So in this chapter, I'm going to walk you through three steps to win over your boss. This will lead to more impact and more income. When your boss knows that he or she can trust you because you're a reliable team member, then it's only natural that your income will increase. You will be given more responsibility, and therefore you will have more opportunity.

Sabotaging or backstabbing your boss is like cutting down a tree while you're climbing it. It's illogical. Whatever your feelings are about your current boss, he or she is the one who has the power to make your work life better or worse.

Some of the biggest mistakes I've ever made professionally were when I put the work I was doing over the priorities of my boss. The reality is, you might be doing work you weren't originally hired to do. Your job might be experiencing scope creep, in which the work you do on a regular basis is very different than what you've been trained to do. So hear me clearly on this: you have one job. Your job is to make your boss look awesome. Here's how to figure out what your boss really wants. Most bosses are easy to figure out if you just pay attention. And here's what you'll discover: bosses have to think differently than their employees. They have to report sales numbers to their manager or the company owner or the board of directors or stockholders. They have to keep customers and clients happy. They need to work with you and your colleagues, making sure the team is running efficiently and moderately getting along with each other.

They have to keep the lights on. The last thing they need is another headache. The last thing they need is for you to not do your job. What they prefer is for you to do your job and also help them do their job. And ideally, your job contributes to one of the key areas they're responsible for. If one of their main jobs is to keep clients happy, and you work with clients on a daily basis, one of the best things you can do is keep your clients happy. That way, your clients never have to complain to your boss. When you show up and do what needs to be done, it benefits not only your clients but also your boss.

Beyond serving your clients, there are areas in the business that you can easily help your boss manage and maintain. There could be systems and processes that could be slightly improved based on your point of view. You might be are aware of situations in your area that your boss might not see on a regular basis. When you bring a different level of intention, doing what you can to serve your boss—and effectively, the whole company—it will make his or her life a lot easier.

If you feel your boss doesn't understand or appreciate your value, or the workplace feels like a battle of wills between you and your boss, then you may want to focus on changing that dynamic. I want you to imagine how it would feel to be a people-first team member, to see your boss's perspective and support your boss's vision for the company. Take some time to see through the eyes of your boss.

See the True Purpose of Your Job

One frustrating trait of our modern-day workforce is when the job description and the actual work doesn't match up. This is a complaint I've heard frequently in my coaching practice. You may have been hired for a position and over time been given more responsibility, until your job shifted to a new position. The first step is to evaluate why you were asked to take on more responsibility that doesn't fit with what you were hired to do. What value does the work you are doing bring to the company? How can you clarify the expectations that your boss has for you?

Help Your Boss Win the Day

You may not want to hear this, but it is an important truth. Your real job is not confined to your initial job description. Your real job is to help your boss win the day. Your job is helping your boss succeed.

Depending on the size of your company, this could get complicated. You may have a direct supervisor looking for one thing from you, and someone superior to that person wanting something completely different. You must navigate both of these relationships. Who is more important? The first person you serve is the manager right above you. I have learned this the hard way. Make them look like a rock star. Do what you can to deliver for them. That is your number one goal. Think of how you can make their life easier. Be the kind of team member they can rely on. It takes just as much (if not more) energy to fight your boss than to deliver exceptional results. What if you were to step up for the next ninety days and really own it, really deliver beyond expectations? Things would change for you.

See Things from His Perspective

Your boss has a lot on his plate. He has a lot on his mind. He's not only thinking about managing you and your team members; he's also thinking about serving the needs of his own boss, the company owner, the board of directors, and the company's clients. If you think about it, your boss has many bosses. This is what makes leadership so difficult.

Be an Incredible Employee

No matter how you've acted or treated your boss in the past, every day can be a new beginning. You can become his trusted advisor, his go-to employee. I say with certainty and confidence that it is better to have a bad boss who trusts you and counts on you than a good boss who doesn't. This may be hard, but there's a season for everything. A season of challenge, a season of training, a season of change. What can you do to really step up and become an incredible employee during this season? Then you'll be able to move forward with integrity. You likely won't have the same boss for your entire career, but you will regret knowing you let your boss get to you and didn't do your best.

A new boss won't fix your problems. Instead focus on fixing the problems that trouble your boss. What if you knew your time was limited and you had only three months? What would it mean to finish strong? If you had only three months left at your current job, what would it mean to bring your best? What can you change today to step up?

Change your performance, but don't announce your change. Let your dedication speak for itself.

Imagine if today were your first day on the job. What would you do differently?

Ideas to Consider

- Your job is to help your boss succeed.
- No matter your current work circumstances, you can choose to be engaged in your work.
- You have the power to change your mindset and habits regarding the tasks before you.
- Your boss's perspective is different than yours.

Actions to Take

- Approach your job as if you were a new employee.
- Take time to see things through your boss's eyes.
- Focus on your boss's priorities.
- As you prepare for work, focus on making today your best day ever. Not tomorrow, not next week, but today!

Home

The Important People We

Too Often Neglect

I heard the thump in the middle of the night. It was a distinct sound—a small body hitting the cold wooden floor. The screams of my two-year-old son started just seconds later. In a dazed and tired state, we put him back in bed, but his pain persisted. He'd sleep for an hour, then wake up in pain. I couldn't sleep. After checking on him several times, I was hit with a realization. He hadn't moved all night. This was my worst nightmare becoming a reality. We tried our best to wait until the morning, but I couldn't shake the fear that my happy, running, giggling son may have taken his last step. We called 911 and the ambulance arrived. Paramedics slid his small frame onto a stretcher that was much too big. There was still no movement from the neck down. They wrapped his tiny body in towels and blankets to protect him from the bumpy dirt road we had to travel to the hospital.

As I followed just fifty feet behind the ambulance transporting my little boy to the hospital and contemplated his potential spine injury, the day's agenda faded into a distant memory. Clients, colleagues, and customers were now eclipsed by this immediate need.

When tragedy strikes, time freezes. The core of who we are

is revealed. Our best and worst behaviors are on display for all to see. We turn to faith, family, and friends to sustain us through the unknown as we wait for news and next steps.

It's times like these when we are reminded, in a way that we feel deep in our gut, that our lives are not about profit or even discovering our purpose; we find our validation and purpose in serving our people. Especially when it is hard. Caring for a sick mother. Being present for a rebellious child. Comforting a grief-stricken coworker. People have a way of outshining our to-do lists.

Once everything is stable again, we lose sight of what was so temporarily important. We binge-watch that new TV show online. We get absorbed in a sporting event or a concert performance. All the luxurious trappings of modern life seem to squeeze out the consideration we have for the people we couldn't live without. If only there were a way to reconcile the clear priorities that emerge in tragedy and the certainty we feel when all is well. How do we stay as equally grounded in the normal and the mundane as we become during the tragic and tense?

It all comes back to people. They are the starting point of everything you want to experience, to have, and to love. Our lives are empty without the people who make it full.

After hours of X-rays and tests, the doctors confirmed that the only consequence of my son's fall was a broken collarbone and a sore neck. Moments after the diagnosis, after we texted our family and friends, everything went back to normal. I checked Instagram. Refreshed my email. Scheduled a conference call.

Many business books have little or nothing to say about home life. They're supposed to be about business, right? But we live multifaceted lives, and all of these "facets" connect and affect each other. Though we may excel at compartmentalizing, in times of tragedy our spouse and kids take precedence over our business. As parents, we drop everything when our kids are sick or hurt. Tension in our marriage affects our ability to focus and perform well in our work. Our people matter.

In the next few chapters, I'll reveal the best strategies I've learned in sixteen years (and counting!) of marriage and share wisdom mined from those who have been married even longer. We'll also talk about kids, addressing some of the challenges to leaving a legacy while trying to keep the lights on. Our home life affects our work, and vice versa. Because it's all about people.

Ideas to Consider

- When your people need you, other to-dos fall to the wayside.
- The core of who you are is revealed in crisis situations.
- Your priorities are revealed when your people need you.
- Your people make your life full; prioritize them.

CHAPTER 6

Spouse

From Kryptonite to Superpower

What if you already have access to the best-kept secret that will build and refine your personal and professional success—indeed, you've had it all along? That secret is your spouse. So many of the entrepreneurs and employees I coach believe that their spouse is the enemy of their dreams. They feel trapped, caught in the hurry of the every day, with bills to pay and mouths to feed. And they mistakenly believe that their days of dreaming are done. "I could never talk about my goals with my husband," a coaching client recently told me. "We are just so busy, and he would never understand." But my friends, your spouse is not the enemy of your dreams. He is not your Achilles' heel. She is not your kryptonite. Instead your spouse can become your secret superpower. I truly believe—and have experienced it for myself—that you can be better together.

In this chapter, you'll do the hard but necessary work of recognizing and responding to the underlying work-home conflict holding you back from your profitable purpose. First, let's identify where your relationship is when it comes to accomplishing your dreams. Here are the four stages most couples progress through in the development and connection of their marriage relationship when they are trying to reach their goals. Read through the descriptions to see where you are with your spouse.

Same Pain

Stage one is identifying the same pain. It's acknowledging an existing pain in your relationship. If you constantly fight about money, the first step is to acknowledge you both feel pain about money. You must recognize there's a problem, and recognition is the first step toward a solution. Maybe you're both feeling stretched too thin and overscheduled. Identifying "overscheduled" as the same pain is the first step in making a change.

Same Page

Stage two is making sure you're both on the same page. This is where you decide together what you want your life to look like. Acknowledging you're stretched too thin and overscheduled is one thing, but dreaming about what you actually want your life to look like is something else. Have an honest conversation so you align your values. I highly recommend choosing a book or an online course to guide you as you move out of your pain and onto the same page.

Same Plan

Stage three is having the same plan. Now that you have both acknowledged where you are and identified where you want to go, it's time to pick your plan. Following the plan will help get you where you want to go and will help unify you as a couple, because you'll be collaborating on each step you take as you move forward.

Same Power

Stage four is having the same power. This is where it gets exciting. You've moved out of the pain and onto the same page and are following the same plan. Things accelerate when you have the same power. You're walking in step with each other, checking in with each other, and encouraging each other. This is an opportunity to really be connected and celebrate your progress along the way. As I look back over my marriage, the times we felt closely connected were when we were living in the same power and working together toward a common goal.

A single Clydesdale horse can pull a load of up to eight thousand pounds. Imagine what happens when we harness two of these horses together. If one Clydesdale can pull eight thousand pounds, then two can pull sixteen thousand pounds, right? Wrong. Two Clydesdales working together can actually pull twenty-four thousand pounds, three times as much weight as either working individually. And there's more! If the two horses have trained as a team and have worked together before, they can pull thirty-two thousand pounds, or four times the weight either could pull on their own.[1] An intentional marriage can create results exponentially more powerful than each spouse can generate on their own.

"If you're a successful person in relationship with another successful person, you've embarked on one of the greatest quests in all human endeavor. For me, it's the ultimate thrill ride, a journey in which every moment is packed with learning potential and the opportunity to experience true joy."[2]

Meet the Millers

Dan and Joanne Miller live on a small farm in Franklin, Tennessee. Dan is a career coach, bestselling author, and conference speaker. His podcast, *48 Days to the Work You Love*,[3] has been a favorite of mine for several years. The Millers have figured out how to live and work together successfully. They are an inspiration to thousands of other young entrepreneurial couples trying to figure out how to pursue their dreams while being married and raising kids. Dan often shares this quote: "The master in the art of living makes little distinction between his work and his play, his labor and his leisure, his mind and his body, his information and his recreation, his love and his religion. He hardly knows which is which. He simply pursues his vision of excellence at whatever he does, leaving others to decide whether he is working or playing. To him he's always doing both."[4]

From personal experience, I can say this is true of the Millers. Joanne is an incredible artist and author. But the two of them aren't

---

1   Jim Stovall, "Horse Sense," GetMotivation, www.getmotivation.com/motivationblog/ 2012/06/horse-sense-by-jim-stovall/.
2   Gay Hendricks, *The Big Leap: Conquer Your Hidden Fear and Take Life to the Next Level* (San Francisco: HarperOne, 2009), 194.
3   Dan Miller, "48 Days Podcast," 48 Days, www.48days.com/listen/.
4   Lawrence Pearsall Jacks, *Education through Recreation* (London: McGrath and National Recreation and Park Association, 1932), 1.

going in separate directions; instead she supports Dan in pursuing his highest calling and his best dream. Dan does the same for Joanne. They have found a way to live, love, and work together. They're not perfect, but they've continued to move toward their ideal life, and they've gotten pretty close. Their model of knowing yourself, learning about your spouse, and supporting each other's dreams as you live a life of service to others is possible for you as well.

Before I met Dan and Joanne, I didn't think it was possible to combine work I loved with a fully engaged family life. I had always envied couples who worked well together. Julie and I had our own tracks when it came to the work we did. We were both teachers before our kids were born. I had my classroom and she had hers. We worked near each other but not with each other. This kind of separation is common in marriages.

But separation can have a dark side. It can be tempting to hide difficulties at work from your spouse, and it doesn't take long to develop unhealthy coping mechanisms as outlets for stress. These look different for everyone: increased time playing video games or visiting social media sites, an extra drink at night, or a flirtatious relationship with a coworker. The distance between you and your spouse widens, and the creek becomes a canyon. Turning away from your spouse becomes a self-fulfilling prophecy. "He would never understand me" leads to "I could never tell him." And the damage seems irreparable.

According to Dan Miller, one of his most popular PDF downloads is about how to deal with a negative spouse.[5] You might feel like your spouse doesn't support your dreams and is quick to tell you why something won't work. You might even be hiding this book, not wanting your spouse to know that you secretly dream of quitting your job and starting an online business (or whatever your secret dream is). I can relate.

---

5   Dan Miller, "5 Tips for Dealing With a Negative Spouse," 48 Days (January 2, 2017), www.48days.com/download/5-tips-dealing-negative-spouse/.

Instead what if you were to imagine your spouse as your secret weapon? Envision the relief of being on the same page together. Picture your spouse as the biggest supporter of your dreams. What if you didn't hide your dreams anymore but chose to share new ideas with your spouse first? Imagine if, instead of being the kryptonite that weakens you and prevents you from reaching your highest goals, your spouse were your superpower, helping you live in the fullness of your potential.

Sound impossible? Know this for sure: the influence of your spouse as your kryptonite or your superpower is largely dependent on your attitude and actions. Your spouse really can be your biggest supporter, your advocate, your encourager, and your teammate as you *both* move toward a life of profitable purpose.

Before we continue, I want you to take a breath. Pause and consider what it would mean to you, and your dream, if you and (your spouse's name) were on the same page. Forget what may be true right now, and imagine what could be.

Imagine If This List of Ten Characteristics Were True of Your Marriage

1. I share my dreams openly with my spouse.
2. When I'm worried about money, relationships, or the future, I tell my spouse, even when I don't yet have a solution.
3. My spouse helps me sharpen my ideas and brings clarity and direction to my vision.
4. He or she is the first one I text when something awesome happens in my work life.
5. My marriage fulfills me, and I'm proud to be married to my spouse.
6. I don't hide the real me from my spouse. He or she knows who I really am.

7. I'm free to share industry talk with my spouse, and my spouse seems interested.
8. Other people wish they had a marriage like ours.
9. I'm free to have bad ideas, and my spouse accepts me anyway.
10. My business and professional life are better because of my spouse's support.

Oh, to dream. What would your life be like if all of the foregoing statements were true, or even if half were true? I have some good news, friend! It's possible. Julie and I have worked hard to get to this point. And though we're by no means the perfect couple, I can honestly say that this list is often true of our marriage. These statements can be true for you as well.

Revisit the list and give each statement a score from zero to ten, based on how true it is of your marriage (with zero being not true at all, and ten being very true). Then add your scores and write the total here: _____.

Now let me show you three tools that will get you closer to a perfect score. Discovering your profitable purpose starts with being unified with your spouse. I've seen too many couples pursuing their individual dreams without that umbrella of unity, sitting in the same relational boat and rowing as hard as they can in two different directions. If you're serious about pursuing a profitable purpose, these three tools will help ensure your spouse becomes your superpower and not your kryptonite.

Pray Together

Simple, right? Listen, I understand if you want to skip this part, if you're not a person of faith or if your spouse is more spiritual than you. But I have to tell you, nothing unifies a married couple more than praying together.

As a leader in my church, I've often heard from couples who have a tough time praying together. They complain they don't have any time, it's too intimate, they don't know what to say, or they aren't on the same page spiritually. I agree. It can be tough. But the effort is worth it. It took me ten years to develop a daily prayer habit with Julie, so I get it. But it is so much easier than you think. Here are a few ways to establish this habit.

First, go to bed together at the same time. I have found that lying in bed is the easiest place to pray together.

Second, hold your spouse's hand and ask what they would like you to pray for. You literally say, "What would you like me to pray for tonight?" And then just wait.

Then simply pray. I know that one sounds easy, but friends often tell me this is the hardest part, so I'm going to give you a script. After they tell you what they want you to pray for, simply close your eyes and say,

Dear God. Thank you for my spouse. Thank you for my family. I pray for (whatever they said). Amen.

That's it. And of course you can always add a few more things before the amen.

Now, there may be an order that works better for you. But in any case, I've found that praying together is a great way to end the day. (Note: Be fairly warned. Praying together as a couple often leads to greater intimacy.)

Make it a habit.

I had to do this for months before it began to feel normal. Now, years later, before I fall asleep, I reach my hand over to Julie's and pray. Every single night. Habits take time. Commit to pray with your spouse for the next thirty days, and you'll begin a habit that could and should last a lifetime. Do it so often that it becomes weird when you don't.

What if you travel? If you travel for work, it's actually even easier. All you do is call your spouse before you go to sleep or before they go to sleep, depending on time zones, and ask, "Would you mind if I pray for us?" Far from minding, I think, any spouse would be thrilled to hear those words. You then say,

Dear God. Thanks for my spouse. Thanks for my family. Please give me a safe trip home. Amen.

A special word for those who travel for work: Affairs happen on the road after ten o'clock. Instead of one more drink at the hotel bar, go to your room, call your spouse, pray with them, and go to bed. You can always get an early start on work in the morning.

In my experience, praying with my spouse has been the single biggest contributor to any success I've had as a business owner, husband, and father.

Create and Read Their Manual

What if you knew exactly what it takes to get the best out of your spouse? What if you knew the secret code to unlocking their greatest strengths, building an authentic connection with them, really dialing in on their love and admiration for you? Wouldn't you want to know the secret?

The second tool for joining together with your spouse and unifying in your pursuit of profitable purpose is to read their manual. Let me explain what I mean by that. Obviously, your spouse doesn't come with a manual, so you need to study them and write your own. The person you are married to now is not the same person you married. They have changed. Kids, age, and the stress of being married to you has changed them. You need to learn again who they are. Until you do this, you aren't going to be able to fully benefit from your spouse's strengths. Fortunately, there are some proven, powerful methods of helping you get to know who they really are.

If you are skeptical about personality tests, I get it. I don't want to be too formulaic in my approach to relationships either. After all, people still have the power of personal choice. With that being said, I have found that tests help us to understand someone's natural tendencies. This knowledge will help you anticipate

- How he or she is most likely to respond in a given situation
- What kind of communication he or she will need in order to make an informed decision
- Whether he or she will need extra time to process a new idea
- What the main intention behind his or her words is, especially when the words are critical

Knowing the answers to these questions has been a lifesaver for my marriage. Among dozens of personality inventories and learning style assessments, I've narrowed the list to my four favorites (and provided some added details in the bonus resources section of this book).

1. Love Languages = how to give and receive love from your partner
2. Enneagram = how you unconsciously see the world and view your relationships
3. Kolbe = how you instinctively take action
4. StrengthsFinder = what makes you gifted

Although there are others, these four tests have stuck with me over time. They will provide more than enough information about your spouse without sending you into an endless cycle of information gathering. I also use them frequently with my colleagues and clients to gain insight about how best to communicate with each individual.

I understand that navigating these tests can be overwhelming. But this is an investment in one of the most important relationships in your life. Knowing the how and why behind your spouse's actions and responses gives you huge relational insights that can influence your choices and conduct.

I'm challenging you to study their manual. How? Take these four tests together and get to know how your spouse sees the world, what they are naturally good at, how they receive love, and what makes them awesome. They will feel heard, valued, and connected to you in ways you never thought possible.

If you are reluctant about investing time and energy into learning about your spouse, let me assure you, nothing is more important. No business deal, job transfer, entrepreneurial idea, or technology is more important than a lifelong, on-the-same-page, committed marriage.

If you are going through a tough time in your marriage right now, a lot of this can seem impossible. I want you to know that I am standing with you. I have seen even the most fractured relationships experience healing when each partner made the choice to take responsibility for the state of their union. No matter how hopeless your current situation may feel, there's always something that can be done. Tiny hinges swing big doors. You never know how these small actions will add up to large life change. So for now, take 100 percent responsibility for your relationship. Follow the principles outlined in this chapter, and you may very well be surprised at the results you experience.

Depending on the difficulty of your current situation, it may be time to bring in a trusted third party, such as a marriage counselor or spiritual advisor. Even the healthiest marriages benefit from an occasional checkup.

Value Their Counsel

The third tool for turning your spouse from your kryptonite into your superpower is valuing their counsel. I am shocked when I hear friends say they

- Bought a house without telling their wife (it's happened twice)
- Took a job out of state without telling their wife (four times)
- Quit their job without telling their wife (ten or more times)
- Lost their job without telling their wife (thirty or more times)

Your spouse sees something in you that you might not see in yourself. They have valuable perspective to share with you. Just like a mirror shows you when your tie is crooked or when you have a piece of spinach stuck in your teeth, your spouse can help you see obvious flaws and improve your ideas to discover your profitable purpose. While you may not always appreciate their timing or technique, this is something you can learn to not only accept but also lean into and trust.

To value your spouse's counsel, you need to do three things.

1. Ask for Their Feedback

Initially this is really hard, and it feels pretty scary. And you can make all the excuses in the world, like, "What will they have to say, anyway? They don't know my industry. I don't trust their advice. They're not good at these kinds of things. It'll probably just freak them out." But whatever excuse you're using, your spouse knows you better than you know yourself. You can't read your own label, but they can read it. They've known you for a long time and have learned your tendencies, preferences, and inclinations. When you ask them for feedback, you are showing them that their perspective matters. This will change them. Trust me. When you begin to include them, not grudgingly but willingly, it will transform them from your kryptonite to your superpower.

2. Listen without Defensiveness

Imagine this: Before leaving the house in the morning, you say, "Honey, I have a big meeting today, and I'm wondering if you have any advice for me?" You might have to ask a few times before they're willing to share what they really think. But when they do, listen. Don't interrupt. Don't defend. Don't object. Just listen. It may take time for the two of you to figure out your rhythm. But it is worth the effort.

3. Report the Results

This is the most important part. It will be like your little secret and will bring the two of you closer together. After the meeting, give your spouse a call. Tell them how it went. They'll feel included in the process. Your spouse is your secret superpower; include them in your work.

After sixteen years of marriage, I can testify that this is one of the best parts. Being able to celebrate with your spouse after you've included her in the process is a great joy. Going out to dinner to celebrate landing that big client that he helped you craft the pitch for is so much fun. Buying her a bouquet of flowers to thank her for the insight she gave you to improve your presentation before the board meeting can show that you truly care. Writing him a short text message letting him know that his suggestions worked can mean the world!

People love to be recognized for their contribution, and this is doubly true for your spouse. Too often, we can take our spouse for granted, but that's exactly why it's so meaningful when we celebrate accomplishments together. When you start with your people, you recognize your home team. You wouldn't be where you are without them. Taking some time to celebrate with your spouse can unify the two of you like never before.

Ideas to Consider

- Know yourself, learn about your spouse, and support each other's dreams.
- You can live in your excuses, or you can have the results you dream of.
- No business deal, job transfer, entrepreneurial idea, or technology is more important than a lifelong, on-the-same-page, committed marriage.
- A solid, committed relationship in which both parties are on the same team starts with your actions and behaviors.
- Recognize how your spouse's differences help fill your gaps, making your ideas stronger.
- The togetherness of prayer encourages intimacy, fosters trust, and builds on the cohesiveness of a team effort.

Actions to Take

- Commit to pray with your spouse for the next thirty days.
- With your spouse, work through different personality inventories and learning style assessments (Love Languages, Kolbe, Enneagram, StrengthsFinder) to better understand each other.
- Develop the habit of asking your spouse for their feedback.

CHAPTER 7

Kids

From Liability to Legacy

I t was one of those nights when I felt like I couldn't get anything done. I had a big project due, and yet it seemed like every five minutes, the kids needed something from me. From bath time and bedtime to brushing teeth and reading stories, the entire night seemed to drag on. When I trudged downstairs to start my work, the messy kitchen seemed to mock me. How was it possible to use so many dishes in just one day?

When I finally sat down to get started, my sleepy daughter appeared at the bottom of the stairs.

"Daddy, I'm hungry," she said. I sighed. After a snack and another good night song, I was back in front of my computer.

Ten minutes later, I heard the horrifying sound of a child choking. I raced upstairs. This time, it was my seven-year-old son throwing up his entire dinner. I cleaned the bathroom, changed the sheets, comforted him, and laid him back down.

On the way back to my computer, I peeked at the baby monitor. Our youngest son, only a year old, was still awake. There was only one thing this could mean: diaper change! Frustrated that I was never going to get to that major project, I bolted up the stairs again and hurriedly changed his diaper. Rushing to leave his room, I heard his sweet voice mutter one syllable that both elated me and slapped me right across the face.

"Dad."

Dad. That is who I am.

Yes, I'm a business owner. Yes, I'm a speaker and an author. Yes, I'm a husband and a friend. But I am also a dad.

If you have kids, you know what this tension is like. As soon as you find out a baby is on the way, your world shifts on its axis. Gravity changes. You were once weightless. Now you are tethered forever. No matter what else happens in your life, the highest highs and the lowest lows, the biggest business success or the most crippling illness, your relationship with your kids will live on.

They are your new gravity, continually pulling you toward the center of your life. And just like the effects of gravity, they can feel like a burden, like an extra weight, an invisible force pulling you back down to earth and preventing your dreams from taking flight.

Before children, all of my time was mine. I could stay up until three in the morning, working on a project, with very few consequences. Saturdays were my day to do whatever I wanted. Most afternoons were completely up to my choosing.

And let's not get started on money. Any money that came into my world was mostly mine. Sure, some went to the government, some went to my church, but the rest was mine for Julie and me to share. We could do whatever we wanted. We could go wherever we wanted. Nothing was holding us back.

Then we became parents and everything changed. We traded trips to the wine bar for trips to Walmart. Buca di Beppo became

Buy Buy Baby. Enjoying fresh bruschetta at Trattoria i Trulli became finding baby wipes in the Target aisle.

There is only so much I can cover in one chapter on kids, so I'm going to rest on one truth that will serve as a through line: Your kids do not have to be a liability. Instead, they can become your legacy. Rather than being a reason why not, they can become a reason why. Your dreams matter because of your children, not in spite of them.

But I get it. Kids seem to get in the way of living out your profitable purpose. Yesterday I needed to spend one extra hour finishing a work project, but then I looked at the clock and saw it was five. I had promised my son that we would do a stop-motion animation project together, so I texted my client and pushed the project back a day. "Can we reschedule? I'm on kid duty."

Then there are all those times I've tried to enjoy a few minutes of peace and quiet. I used to hate errands, but now I willingly volunteer, because solitude is bliss. As I'm on my way out the door, the last thing I want to hear is Julie saying, "Can you take a kid with you?"

But if you have kids, they will always tag along. This is part of the responsibility of parenting. Children require constant adult supervision and affection.

Your kids are looking to you, so your work, attitude, and habits matter. They're learning habits and behavior from you.

What if you could thrive in your parenting as you pursue your profitable purpose? What if the forced limitation of children were actually a hidden asset?

Recognize the Power of Limitations

Instead of a disadvantage, your children can become your productivity machines. They force you to use your time to the highest efficiency because it's so limited. In a world of decision fatigue caused by too many distractions and choices, your children are your strategic advantage. You simply don't have the luxury of being distracted.

Instead of fighting gravity, rely on it. Think about this: most sports rely on gravity. There is power in limitation! The ball being dunked into the hoop. The kick going through the uprights. The home run knocked out of the park. Gravity is what makes these sports fun. Rather than denying the gravity of being a parent, learn to use this limitation as a filter to help clarify your most important actions.

You may be familiar with Parkinson's law, which states that the amount of time a task takes is equal to the amount of time you allocate for that task. If you have thirty days to move, it will take you thirty days. But if you find out that your dream house is available in just two days, you'll find a way to make it work and move in just two days. Another familiar concept is the Pareto principle, known as the 80/20 rule, which states that 80 percent of your results will come from 20 percent of your efforts.

Parkinson's law means that the time you have for tasks after children dramatically shrinks. Add the Pareto principle, and instead of 20 percent of your efforts leading to 80 percent of your results, you don't even have 100 percent of your time. You have only 15–20 percent of your time, so your efforts need to yield the best results.

Having kids automatically limits the time you have available. I'm drafting this chapter on a walk with my youngest son. But I have learned to leverage our stroller-walking time to maximize my writing results. If I have only an hour to write a chapter, then that chapter will take only an hour.

What if you look at your limited capacity of just an hour or two of free time per day, likely after the kids are in bed, and you get your best work done? Your children can help set you apart, because you have clarity of purpose and limited availability. Yes, there will be nights when it seems like nobody wants to go to bed. There'll be seasons when it just seems like you can't find a minute to yourself. But there is joy in the journey. And there's opportunity within the limitations.

Set the Tone of Your Home

Your kids pick up a lot of subtle things from you and put them in their quiver of resources: your voice, your attitude, your demeanor, your vocabulary, the way you talk about people—all of that is setting a norm for them. It's tuning their ears for what is normal, and that's something that will continue the rest of their lives. Your voice is a soundtrack that will play in their ears forever. They're learning from you. What does it mean to be a spouse? What's the right view of money? What does it look like to show up when something is hard? What does it look like to take care of responsibilities even when it's not convenient?

At work, it's up to your clients or your boss or even the industry that controls much of your day to set the day's tone. But at home, you get to make the decision. You decide how busy you will be with sports. You decide how important a morning and evening routine is. You decide what kind of media you're going to allow inside your home.

Your kids grow up believing that the way you taught them is the way it should be. From a very early age, they're learning the tones of home. They're learning what it means to be in tune with the notes you're teaching them.

Even as they grow older and enter their teenage and postcollege years, your kids will continue to look back to your home as the place where they learned their identity and began to express themselves.

That is monumental. You have an incredible opportunity. In all of my years in education, both as a teacher and as a school administrator, I knew that my impact would never be as great as that of my students' parents and their home environment.

So of course when we start with our people, it includes our kids. You get to decide what your home is going to feel like, and it changes everything.

Introducing the Life Calculator

A few years ago, I was approaching a milestone birthday and created a little exercise. I was looking at our family budget, and I decided to open up a new tab on my Google spreadsheet. I wrote the year at the top, on the next row down I wrote my current age, on the row below that I wrote the income from my tax return, and then in the following rows I wrote the ages of our kids. In the next column, I wrote my age the next year, the ages of my kids the next year, and my income plus 10 percent. And then I continued these columns all the way over until my eighty-fifth birthday. On just one screen, I was able to look at the ages of my kids at milestone birthdays and how old I will be in that year. It was also interesting to see what I'll be making at the retirement age of sixty or sixty-five if my income grows by 10 percent each year.

This exercise is very sobering. It made me realize the following.

- The future is a debt. The future is coming whether you like it or not, and there will be expenses to pay. I go more into this in the money mindset chapter, but it is sobering to look at how many years there are for me to save up for my daughter's wedding. How many years ahead until my kids need college funds. How many years until my retirement. There are not as many as I might like!
- Kids are not going to be their current age forever. This exercise also really challenged me to see them for who they are today. Every day they are growing. They are getting older. I need to take advantage of my opportunities today.

■ Then finally it was encouraging. If I keep working hard, if I keep putting my clients' needs before my own, my income will continue to grow. And over time, that growth is significant. The opportunities are endless.

You can download a copy of the Life Calculator at *startwithyourpeople.com/life*.

Train Them according to Their Bent

Don't make your artist an athlete. Parenting expert Danny Silk explains that we need to become students of who our kids are.[1] Every child is different. They have different interests, skills, personality types, and physical characteristics. I've taught and led more than three thousand students during my fourteen years in K–12 education. And I never met a student who was a carbon copy of another student. I even taught three different sets of twins, and they were more different than many of the other students in my class.

Get to Know Your Kids

Your kids are different from you. They're different from their siblings. They're different from their friends. Every child is unique. If you want to start with your people, you can do no better than learning your child in your own home. To train your child according to the way they are made means learning their natural inclinations. This concept can be particularly tricky for high-achieving parents who have kids who don't have the same skills. We start with our

---

1   Danny Silk, *Loving Our Kids on Purpose* (Shippensburg: Destiny Image, 2008), 64.

people. We learn the skills and strengths of each of our children. We don't give up on teaching them; we focus on learning their natural strengths and helping them accentuate those advantages. As Einstein has been credited as saying, "Everybody is a genius. But if you judge a fish by its ability to climb a tree, it will live its whole life believing that it is stupid."

Knowing the love language of my three kids is really helpful in the way that I talk and interact with them. In his book *The 5 Love Languages of Children*, Dr. Gary Chapman explains that "every child has a special way of perceiving love" and that "speaking your child's primary love language will meet his or her deep emotional need for love."[2] My five-year-old daughter Emmaline's love language is physical touch. She feels loved when I wrestle with her. My eight-year-old son Ryland's love language is acts of service. He feels loved when I do something for him, like change batteries or set up his Legos. Even if I teach him something as part of an act of service, he feels loved. He doesn't need hugs like Emmaline does, but he wants to know that Daddy is helping him. My son Hudson is still really young, so we haven't quite figured out his love language yet, although it seems to be quality time. He can be clingy when he really wants us to spend time with him. We'll find out more when he's a little older.

Speak Life into Your Children

Every night before turning out the light, say, "I love you. I'm proud of you. You're good at X." I want the last words my children hear before they go to bed to be a reinforcement of their identity. As a dad, I know that my presence in my kids' lives will be either a bright

---

2   Gary Chapman and Ross Campbell, *The 5 Love Languages of Children* (Chicago: Moody, 1997), 22.

light or a dark shadow. Using words to encourage them will help brighten their path.

Find Time for Yourself

One of the challenges of having kids is that they need you all of the time. At first, you really do want to spend all your time with them. After all, they're your kids! But eventually you realize you're going to need a break. In my roles as an employer, a mentor, and a friend, I've encountered couples who really struggle to find time for themselves. This is unhealthy for their marriage relationship. You can't be with your kids twenty-four hours a day, seven days a week. Here are three strategies to help you find time for yourself when you are a parent.

1. Establish a Morning Routine

A morning routine can help you set the day right. I find having an hour to myself before any of the kids wake up is enough for me to feel like I have my own life. On the days I wake up at the same time as my kids, I feel behind all day. Waking up an hour earlier requires sacrifice but is always worth it. I've learned that if I want to feel like a person, I need to wake up at least an hour before the kids, which is tough because my five-year-old girl is currently waking up at 6:03 every day. Yep, 6:03. So 5:00 a.m. is my time. I need this time to think, read, write, and breathe.

2. Designate a Kid-Free Zone

It's important to have a kid-free zone in your life. Once you have kids, set boundaries to maintain your mental and physical health, so you can be present with your kids but also deliver on professional commitments. I recommend this be both a physical boundary and a time boundary. For the most part, our kids are not allowed in my home office. I'd recommend you have a place in your house that is off-limits to the kids. As someone who works from home, I've learned that it can be really tricky to find time to myself to have deeper thoughts. I need to have a barrier between my work life and my kids. We have trained the kids to know that when Daddy has the door closed to his office, they are not allowed to enter. It's a really simple rule and required some discipline to implement, but once the kids got it, we never looked back.

3. Set Aside a Weekly Date Night

I intentionally put this tip in the kids' chapter because I believe a great marriage is the best gift you can give your kids. Taking time as a couple without the kids once a week will enable you to have an adult conversation, give you a chance to process what's going on in your life, and let you reflect on where you are as a couple. I have met couples who have gone years without having a kid-free date. Take some time away from your children. It's one of the best tips I can give you when it comes to being an awesome parent.

Ideas to Consider

- See kids as a blessing, not a hindrance to your life. They are your legacy.
- Consider Parkinson's law and the Pareto principle. Leverage your time (with your kids or during down time) to maximize productivity.
- Get to know your children as their authentic selves.

Actions to Take

- Learn your children's love languages.
- Schedule quality time to be with your kids and away from them.
- Invest in your marriage through consistent, kid-free dates.

Life

Find the Balance between

the Have and the Want

In this last part of the people section, we are going to focus on the remaining people in your life. We've covered people at work. We've talked about people at home. But did you know that your friends can be your secret advantage to a life of profitable purpose? I'll explain in the next chapter. After that, I'll walk you through proven strategies for dealing with the difficult people in your life. It's one thing to start with the people you get along with; I'll show you how to navigate the more challenging relationships that you'll inevitably face. Finally, we'll conclude this section by talking about what may very well be your most important relationship—the one between you and the person in the mirror.

CHAPTER 8

Friends

Your Secret Advantage

It looked like just another Friday morning at a coffee shop. The familiar whirr of the espresso machine. The aroma of freshly brewed coffee. A long line of patrons in a hurry to grab their favorite drink and face one more day at the office before the weekend. I was casually sitting at our usual table with a group of my five closest friends. Chatting, laughing, and sharing life together. Definitely not in a hurry. Then I noticed a businessman staring my way.

I nodded politely and leaned back into the conversation at my table. A few minutes later, I looked up to see him towering over us, a cup of coffee in his hand.

"I'm sorry guys, I just have to ask. What are you meeting about?"

Sean was the first one to speak up. "Oh! This is just our mastermind."

"OK. Wait. What?" the businessman replied. "So this isn't a business meeting?"

"No," I replied. "This is just a group of guys trying to help each other level up. We meet every Friday to talk about our struggles and share things that are working. It's my favorite part of the week."

That was the moment I realized that what we had was something rare. This kind of conversation happened multiple times over the next few years. Our weekly mastermind group was a curiosity to people in a hurry to get to work. This group was something special. Our weekly Friday 6:00 a.m. meetups were one of the keys to my success. This group of guys was the support system that saw me through many challenges in both business and life.

I searched the faces of my guys, and we all knew. This weekly time of connection, encouragement, and challenge was our secret advantage. Somehow the word spread. Over the course of the next year, we were approached at least a dozen times by others who wanted to join our group. And when we politely declined, the same questions were asked. "How did you start it? What do you guys talk about? How do I start my own?"

So in this chapter, I'll explain why a mastermind can make all the difference in your success. I'll show you how to find the people who should be in your mastermind, and I'll walk you through the steps of starting one.

What Is a Mastermind?

A mastermind is a group of people dedicated to each other's success. They meet on a regular basis. They share their struggles, celebrate their wins, and set tangible goals. Each member contributes to the lives of the others, with the net effect of helping each other grow in their lives and in their businesses. As Jim Rohn says, "You are the average of the five people you spend the most time with."[1] In a mastermind, you have the opportunity to choose who those influential people will be.

Benefits of a Mastermind

Encouragement

When I'm feeling discouraged, all I need to do is reach out to one of the guys in my mastermind. I know I'll receive the encouragement, feedback, and challenge I need to keep moving forward. Since you are the average of the five people you hang around, make sure these people are on your side, cheering you on and encouraging you both in the struggles and in the triumphs. In a private Facebook group, Sally Hope explained, "I love my mastermind for the support, community, and the varying ideas of people in different industries than me." Katrin Hahner added, "The benevolent and sharp wisdom of the women in my mastermind ALWAYS nudges me beyond my comfort zone and out of fear, self-pity, or playing small. It always helps me to strive for excellence and have more courage and perspective."

Feedback

A mastermind serves as your very own personal board of directors. When you are contemplating a big decision, such as going for a promotion, starting a new project, or handling any number of issues, imagine what it would be like to have a team of high-performing individuals to help you make the right decision. Their feedback is invaluable. My friend Ruth Soukup, an author, explains, "We need

---

1   Jim Rohn, as quoted in Maarten van Doorn, "You Are the Average of the Five People You Spend the Most Time With," *Medium*, June 20, 2018, https://medium.com/the -polymath-project/you-are-the-average-of-the-five-people-you-spend-the-most-time-with -a2ea32d08c72.

truth tellers and naysayers, people who love us enough to call us out when we are going down a bad path and who care enough to get in our face."[2]

A Place to Share Your Wins

Culturally, we've made it taboo to share our successes publicly. Bragging is seen as a bad thing. But not in a mastermind! This is a safe place to say, "Look at what I did! Isn't this awesome?" That's one of my favorite parts of our mastermind. And it's changed the way I look at my goals. With a mastermind, I set goals even higher, knowing that I have trusted friends who will cheer me on along the way and celebrate my achievements. Through the years, I've been able to brag along with my friends. We each have our moment in the sun to celebrate, with no jealousy or envy, just embracing what we've been able to accomplish. Reaching your goal is so much sweeter when you are surrounded by people who are for you and not threatened by you.

A Safe Place to Share Struggles

We all need a safe place to share our struggles. A place where we can be real and we don't have to hide. Each of us has secrets we are holding on to, whether it's a compromising decision at work, fear about our finances, or a moral or personal indiscretion. What would it mean for you to have a few trusted brothers or sisters you could reach out to and be real with?

New Ideas

My mastermind has challenged me to level up in the following ways: Following a particular eating plan for a set amount of days, such

---

2   Ruth Soukup, "Embracing Honest Feedback (Even When It Hurts)," *Do It Scared*, podcast, episode 31, transcript available at https://s3.amazonaws.com/do-it-scared/Transcripts/DIS-+Episode+31+Transcript.pdf.

as Whole30 or the Slow-Carb Diet. Completing physical fitness routines over a set number of days, such as the push-up challenge. They've introduced me to new teachers, books, and concepts that have changed my thinking and opened up new doors of opportunity.

So How Do You Start a Mastermind?

Create a Dream List of People You Want to Invite

The first step in starting a mastermind is to create a list of people you would love to invite. Inviting the right people is the key to a successful mastermind.

My favorite mastermind wasn't even created with a focus on my career. Instead I reached out to four guys in careers other than mine, so we were sort of a network of peers. It was a way for me to get perspective outside of my industry.

Instead of using the same techniques I was familiar with as a classroom teacher and school administrator, I now had an attorney, an entrepreneur, a business coach, and a sales professional, all advising me, explaining how things worked in their industry and helping me level up my business.

Potential mastermind members to consider:

- People in your industry
- People who inspire you
- People outside of your industry
- People from church
- People from work
- People from your local community

Decide on the Logistics

Decide the day and time to meet and whether you'll meet in person or online. If you choose to meet in person, select a location you can count on each week. I've known masterminds that meet at a coffee shop, a conference room, or the house of one of the members. There's something so powerful about being in the same room, even though there can be logistical challenges.

An online mastermind is great because you are not limited to picking people from your area; people from all over the world can participate. If you are meeting online, I highly recommend using Zoom videoconference software. This way, you can not only see each other's faces during the meeting but also record each of your meetings.

Make the Invitation

Now that you've developed your dream list, I recommend inviting people in phases. Start with a few at the top of your list and work down until you've filled your mastermind. And I would aim for seven to ten people as a start. You might consider allowing committed members to invite a friend. If you begin with your top four, and each of them says yes to bringing a friend, you are now at nine—a great number to start with.

Don't worry about people saying no; it may not be a good fit at the time. That's okay.

Here's the email I used to start my mastermind.

Hey guys,

I look up to each one of you for many different reasons.

I would like to invite you to join me in a new adventure—starting a mastermind. A mastermind is a weekly meeting of guys to share what we're learning, what we're working through, as well as provide support and encouragement. I propose that we meet every Friday at 6:00 a.m. at the Starbucks on College Drive. This will lead to business growth and personal growth. If you are interested, just write back. And if you're not, please ignore this email. No hard feelings.

You can watch a video of a few of my mastermind members talking about what it was like to start a mastermind with me at *startwithyourpeople.com/mastermind*.

Run the First Meeting

Start on time, introduce yourself, and explain the purpose of the mastermind. You may say something like this:

> Welcome, everybody. I'm so honored that you are here. The purpose of this mastermind is to meet regularly to share our struggles, cheer on each other's success, and set tangible goals to help us move forward in our life and work. This is a safe place. What you share here stays here. The reason it's called a mastermind is because all of us together are smarter than one of us on our own. And we will be there to support each other when things don't work out.

Although there are as many formats as there are masterminds, here is a model schedule to follow.

- Share your wins (three minutes each).
- Share where you're struggling or one area in which you need help (three to five minutes each).
- Put someone on the hot seat—one member shares a problem in their life or business and asks for feedback and encouragement from the other mastermind members (twenty to forty minutes).
- Share goals for the next meeting (two to three minutes each).

Depending on how many people you have in your mastermind, this could take anywhere from forty-five minutes to an hour or two.

You might also use the following questions to guide your discussion.

1. What was the hardest lesson you learned this week?
2. What is one resource you were glad to discover this week?
3. If you could redo a decision or an action this week, what would it be?
4. What are you worried about for next week?
5. What are you most excited about?
6. What are you too embarrassed to tell us?
7. What's the biggest success you've had this week?
8. Where is there tension in your most important relationships?

Set a weekly day and time in your calendar and ask each member to commit to attending every meeting. Commitment will make the difference between a mastermind that does well and one that stagnates.

Friendship Tracker

Since you are the average of the five people you spend the most time with, here is an exercise to help determine your top five influences. I call this the Friendship Tracker. Here's how it works. Over the course of a week, note in your calendar who you are spending time with. That includes people at work, your spouse, people you know through sports or hobbies, and people you communicate with via text message and social media. What you may realize at the end of the week is that the top five people in your life are not people encouraging you to grow. You may discover that you're spending a lot of time with a negative coworker or an old friend from high school who no longer challenges you. Until you keep track, you will never know who your true friends are.

Two Kinds of Friends

As you review your Friendship Tracker, you may realize that there are two types of friends in your life: growth friends and broken-wing friends.

A growth friend is someone who encourages you to keep growing in your life. They are for you. Each time you speak with them, there's a new book that they are reading. There's a new TED Talk they've recently watched. There's a new idea that they have. They are on your side, and they're challenging you to think bigger about your life.

Then there are the broken-wing friends. These people are constantly talking about things that are broken. They complain about how things are instead of imagining how they could be. These are nonreciprocal relationships, taking much more than they are giving. These people are always looking at the negative. They seem to constantly be facing a challenge.

After a conversation with a growth friend, you feel inspired and encouraged.

After a conversation with a broken-wing friend, you feel drained and worn out.

You likely have both kinds of people in your life. The challenge is in deciding how much time you want to spend with growth friends and how much time you want to spend with broken-wing friends.

We'll always have broken-wing friends. And it's important to be there for people who are hurting. But if we're honest, there are friends who are so negative, so draining, that can discourage us from reaching our goals, sticking to positive habits, or thinking bigger about our lives.

There are broken-wing friends at work with whom you wish you could spend less time.

There are relationships you may never have considered as having a negative impact. They might be coworkers, neighbors, people in various social settings, people from church, parents of other kids, and even (dare I say it?) family members.

If you are dealing with a broken-wing friend, it might be time to move forward or at least put some stronger boundaries in place.

Addressing a Broken-Wing Friend

Walking into the coffee shop, I knew this was going to be a difficult conversation. I approached the table where Sean and Ryan were already seated.

Sean was surprised to see me. We hadn't spoken in months. He knew something was happening but wasn't sure what.

I sat down and Ryan started in. "I love you two guys, and it seems like there's some distance between you. And I think Brian has something he wants to share, so let's talk about it."

I took a deep breath and turned to Sean. "You know, I feel like the way you talk about women is not positive. It's not helpful." I went on to explain to him how his comments about women were degrading and needed to stop.

It was one of the hardest conversations I've ever had.

There was a lot of blame, hurt feelings, and even a few tears. But I'm so glad Ryan was there to help facilitate the conversation. For a while after that meeting, things changed. But over time, Sean fell back into his old routine. I wish this story had a happier ending, but relationships are messy. Sean and I have spoken only once or twice since then. Confronting a broken-wing friend is never easy, but it must be done. You can let time pass, but time does not heal all wounds. Often, time just creates unhealed scars.

I'll admit, this is a difficult journey. It's uncomfortable. But you can live through this. Here's how.

Address the Issue

As Gay Hendricks, author of *The Big Leap* (one of my all-time favorite books), says, "Behind every communication problem is a sweaty ten-minute conversation you don't want to have."[3] So that's where you start. Address the issue one-to-one—ideally, in person. Share your concerns with your friend, trusting and hoping they will be able to hear you.

Bring in a Third Party

If things don't change, it might be a good idea to bring in a third party, a mutual friend who can help facilitate the conversation. Sometimes we don't know how we're coming across to other people, and having someone who can see both sides can really help.

Pause the Relationship

If your friend refuses to meet or to address the issue, it may be time to take a break. This can be challenging, especially in social situations with mutual friends. In extreme cases, it might even require moving or changing jobs. But the future is a long time, and your dreams are worth facing the awkwardness of a difficult situation.

When You Outgrow a Friendship

As you continue to level up your life, grow in business, and build your network, you are going to experience tension with those who are not moving forward. Perhaps friends from school or people you've known a long time are now perceiving your growth as a threat to their life choices. This can be hard to process, because you're excited about where you're going and you want to share

---

3   Gay Hendricks, *The Big Leap: Conquer Your Hidden Fear and Take Life to the Next Level* (New York: HarperOne, 2010), 52.

with them what you are learning. Sometimes you simply outgrow a friendship.

Over the course of my life, I've seen friendships grow and friendships fade, but one thing has remained. The door is open to reconnect in the future. So if the relationship is ending, let them go with grace, encourage them in their goals, and do not judge them according to your path.

Leveling Up Your Life

As we close out this chapter, there are two additional relationships that you may want to consider to help you level up your life.

An Accountability Coach

One of my favorite things I get to do is coach clients one-on-one to help them get clarity in their lives and work. An accountability coach can help you reach new levels of growth. You can learn more about our people-first coaching services at *startwithyourpeople.com/coaching*. As bestselling author Hal Elrod explains, "I got more done in four months with accountability than I did in four years without accountability."[4] I've seen my clients get clarity about their messages, start thriving businesses, and increase their incomes. I'm sure a coach would work for you as well.

A Paid Mastermind

If you really want to level up your life and your business, you might look into a paid mastermind. A paid mastermind is usually hosted by a thought leader such as a speaker, an author, or a course creator

---

4   Hal Elrod, "Beyond the Bestseller with Hal Elrod," podcast interview with Chandler Bolt, Self-Publishing School, July 25, 2017, *https://self-publishingschool.com/sps-013-beyond -bestseller-hal-elrod/*.

and generally lasts for one year. It may cost anywhere between five thousand dollars to twenty thousand dollars per year to be part of this exclusive group. Your fee usually includes weekly group coaching calls, quarterly in-person meetings—at luxurious locations such as spas or resorts—and one-on-one sessions with your coach. The benefit of a paid mastermind is the opportunity to gain the perspective of both the coach and mastermind members for the whole year. Members of a paid mastermind often see results far more quickly in one year together than they would have in five years on their own. You can sign up to receive a notification when my mastermind opens up to new members at *briandixon.com/mastermind*.

Ideas to Consider

- Mastermind groups can be life-changing.
- Mastermind groups are underutilized but for many people can be attainable with fairly straightforward guidelines.
- Often, we aim to be average in our peer groups. Therefore in order to improve ourselves, we need to improve our peer groups.
- We should let go of relationships that discourage us from reaching our goals.

Actions to Take

- Track and evaluate the top five people you spend time with.
- Create a mastermind group and hold your first meeting.
- Have a hard conversation with someone holding you back and prepare for ending the relationship.
- Determine whether the people surrounding you are pushing you to be the best version of yourself.

CHAPTER 9

Difficult People

How to Turn an Adversary

into an Advocate

When we moved to California many years ago, I landed my dream job. I was hired to create and teach a digital media program at a well-funded private school just blocks from the ocean.

I was welcomed warmly by my principal and fellow teachers, given a generous budget to purchase equipment, and trusted with the autonomy I craved in order to create an engaging program for my students. It truly was an incredible opportunity.

Everything seemed perfect. Perfect, that is, until I met Melvin (not his real name). He had been on staff for decades and had found a way to create his own position, with a hand in every pot of the organization. His personality was abrasive and he was often condescending. Since he controlled anything having to do with technology, people were afraid to confront him, for fear they would get an old computer or, worse, be berated in front of their peers. In Melvin's world, there were two kinds of people—friends and idiots. You were never sure which one you were on any given day.

During my first year at the school, I saw students belittled, teachers quit, and good projects die, all because of Melvin.

Over time, I made it my personal mission to stop Melvin. My desire for justice and— I'll admit it now—vengeance led me to find ways to work around him rather than with him. As another school year began, I'd had enough. I was now a teacher technology specialist, and my job was to make sure the teachers knew how to use the technology in their classrooms. When I checked in on one of our brand-new teachers, she expressed frustration about some of the equipment that Melvin had set up in her room.

I walked into her tiny classroom to find a massive box of cords dangling right in the middle of the wall above a student desk. With my limited technical knowledge and without asking anyone for permission (especially Melvin), I grabbed some screwdrivers and started moving the equipment.

Within a few minutes, Melvin came busting through the door, yelling obscenities like a drunken sailor. I was livid. I stepped right up into Melvin's face and let him have it. I unleashed a barrage of words that sent him into a tizzy.

Needless to say, regret immediately set in. I had overstepped my authority and taken matters into my own hands in a very disrespectful way.

The next day, I was called into our human resource director's office and given a letter to sign, admitting my fault. I had no choice but to sign it. The damage had been done, because I had let Melvin get to me.

Melvins are everywhere. There will always be people who break the rules, don't follow protocol, are too uptight, or just make your life difficult. Work would be easier without a Melvin. After ten years, I've learned several lessons about how to work with people like Melvin. And I'm here to share with you what I have learned, to help you work with even the most difficult person.

When you adopt the people-first mindset, conflicts and misunderstandings can be resolved in a way that ensures you can look back and be proud of how you responded.

The way I handled the situation with Melvin is one of my biggest professional regrets. Tragically, just a few years later, Melvin had a serious stroke. I have mourned the way I treated him and have often wished I could go back and do it differently.

In the years since, I have had the opportunity (yes, that's what I see it as now—an opportunity) to work with many more Melvins. It is possible to work with them instead of sinking to their level and saying or doing something you regret.

Imagine what it would be like for you and Melvin to be on the same team. To fight side by side each day for your clients and your customers. To see "we" instead of "you versus me." Because you are already on the same team. If you work together, if you live in the same neighborhood, if you go to the same church, if you're in the same family, you are on the same team. But I get it. Living and working with difficult people can be frustrating and overwhelming. So allow me to share a few strategies for dealing with the difficult people in your life.

Clear the Air

While running the school, whenever I became aware of an issue between me and a team member, I'd try to address the issue as soon as possible. I'd invite him into my office and intentionally sit on the same side of the table, looking at a whiteboard together. I said to them, "It seems like there is some tension between us. I'm here to let you know that I want to help clear the air. I see this as the beginning of the conversation, and I know we might not solve everything today, but I want you to know that I'm here to listen."

That's the first step in clearing the air—hear the grievance.

When there's an issue between you and another person, do your best to go to them directly. Take responsibility for your part and open the floor for others to air their grievance, seeking to understand their perspective and listen to their side.

Involve a Third Party

If someone refuses to meet with you or you can't resolve the issue together, it's time to involve a mutually trusted third party. This may be a superior at your office, a friend you both know, or some other neutral party.

I have found that often just the offer of bringing in the third party gets the situation moving toward a resolution. If you do end up meeting with a third party, be careful not to be defensive, and avoid trying to prove your case. Instead look for ways to find common ground.

Document and Move Forward

If the person is still unwilling to meet with you or a third party, eventually you get to a point where it's time to move forward. Document and move on. Give a clear window to let them know your intentions, and then take action.

I had a situation in which I could not get a client to move forward in deciding on a project.

I had been patient. I had given her months to decide on her next course of action and had suggested that we meet with the agreed-upon third party. She was unresponsive and didn't seem to be looking for a solution. I gave notice that in the next thirty days, I would move forward if I didn't hear back from her. I included a copy of the email to my attorney and the third party. I was able to move forward knowing that I gave her a chance to deal with the issue.

You can't force people to deal with their issues. If you've given them ample opportunity to seek resolution and they are still unresponsive, you can move forward with a clear conscience.

Keep the Door Open

This one is particularly personal for me. Instead of writing somebody off after they haven't communicated or have done something unexplainable, keep the door open for redemption and reconciliation in the future. You just never know what that person is going through. And I've lived long enough to see situations come back around and I finally understand what someone was facing at the time. I've learned repeatedly that showing compassion and keeping the door open is often the most proactive stance you can take. I've heard it said that if we treat people like they are hurting, we will be right 80 percent of the time. Well, I like those numbers. So be compassionate. Don't slam the door on someone just because they didn't handle a situation very well. Be gracious and willing to seek reconciliation even as time passes.

When the Difficult People Are Family

What if the difficult people are related to you? One of the challenges I've seen influential people deal with is not getting support from their family. As they step into their greatness and begin to take big leaps in their career, their success is seen as a threat by those who know them best. Unfortunately, that is often part of the deal. Sometimes you grow beyond your upbringing.

Success often brings critics, and critics can come from the most unexpected places. You may have thought those closest to you would support you, but instead they judge you. They don't see things the way you see them. And this can be tremendously frustrating!

One of the best ways to free yourself from family frustration is to let them be who they are and love them anyway, wherever they are on their journey. It can be easy to cling to expectations that we put on other people, but in reality, the only people we can change are ourselves.

Family issues are some of the most contentious to deal with. Especially as we age, the child-parent relationship can be fraught with misunderstanding, judgment, and unmet expectations. And you may never see eye to eye. But compassion goes a long way. Forgiveness is freedom. Choosing to accept reality by loving what is instead of what could be is a first step to rebuilding a healthy family relationship.

Dealing with Critics

If you have ever gone down the road of trying to appease a critic in an effort to convince them of your perspective, you've likely learned that there really is no winning. If somebody is against you, you are not going to change their mind.

We can be so sensitive to the voice of the critic that it prevents us from taking action at all, because we are too afraid of what other people will say. Instead we need to accept reality and use data to drive our decision.

When your boss or mentor becomes your critic, their jealousy and fear of betrayal is most acute when they are emotionally invested in you. Business strategist David D'Alessandro reminds us to beware the mentor who expects lifetime servitude. The wrong mentor thinks, "How could you possibly rise to my level and keep me awake nights with the fear that someday I might have to work for you?"[1]

How to Win Them Over

Slow down, calm down, breathe in, breathe out. Take your time, but take responsibility.

"If we're not careful, we can make a life-altering decision based on a temporary situation rather than on our values."[2] What you don't deal with today will only get more expensive the longer you wait. Don't give a person permission to change your perception of yourself. Time will tell what's going on in someone's heart. If you are not sure, their true nature will eventually reveal itself.

Don't Assume They Know

Into each of our relationships we bring our own set of expectations. But I have learned that it is not fair for me to assume that people have been taught the same values and behaviors that I learned from my upbringing. This may sound old-fashioned, but my wife and I are doing our best to teach our three kids basic cultural norms—introducing yourself, looking people in the eye, shaking hands, saying please and thank you, leaving a place better than you found it—and our kids are standing out and impressing adults on a regular basis.

When you assume other people should behave the way you were taught, you are projecting your expectations onto them. But

---

1   David D'Alessandro, *Executive Warfare* (New York: McGraw-Hill Education, 2008), 63.
2   John C. Maxwell, *Today Matters* (New York: Warner, 2004), 25.

it is illogical to get frustrated when someone doesn't live up to your standard if you've never communicated it to them. You are only causing yourself pain. The wound is self-inflicted.

I can't assume that those I work with are going to know behaviors and systems that I want them to know. So I need to see it as my job to teach people my expectations and help them understand them. A people-first leader recognizes these gaps and communicates clear expectations to ensure everyone is on the same page.

Make an Effort to Reconcile

Some people won't change, but it doesn't mean we rule them out before we've given them a shot. Is there someone in your life whom you've ruled out? Are they so X (name your particular issue with them) that you don't even want to try anymore? Don't let another day pass without starting the conversation. All we have when we don't resolve an issue is regret. Don't let regret become the story of your past, present, or future.

There are people in your life who need you to see them. There are people right now who have unsettled issues with you. There is something missing. But friend, there is freedom. And there is healing. When you put people first, things begin to change. Relationships can be restored. Enemies can turn into friends. You can move forward with integrity and vision, knowing that you dealt with the difficult parts of life. Unfortunately, it may not be possible to restore every relationship, but there is still freedom in trying.

A Proven Process for Disarming Critics

When I was a school administrator, I was often required to have a difficult conversation with a teacher or parent. Early on, I rearranged my office to accommodate these conversations in a way that led to mutual trust. I removed the conference table and just left a whiteboard and two chairs. When someone entered my office with a complaint, we sat down beside the whiteboard and worked on a solution together. We no longer were in conflict, because we were on the same side of the room. It was the whiteboard that we had an issue with. The whiteboard was where we put our problems. The whiteboard was where we put our unmet expectations. And because we wrote it down, we could always clean it up. Agreeing on the challenge and writing it down is the first step in finding a solution.

I'd start the meeting by saying, "It seems like we're having a challenge, and my goal is to understand your perspective and to make sure that I hear you out regarding your issues so that we can work on solving them together."

Starting the meeting this way was often disarming. People felt like they had already been understood, because I was seeking to understand. As soon as they started talking, I said, "Oh, do you mind if I write it down?" And they almost always said, "No, that's fine" and then continued talking, and I wrote key words and ideas on the board.

I have to admit, it felt strange at first. But when someone said, "I don't feel heard," I wrote on the board, "Doesn't feel heard." If they said, "I'm really frustrated because of the timing," I wrote down, "Timing." Each issue was written until everything was on the whiteboard.

Once the person had finished stating their frustrations, I asked, "Is there anything else? When you look at this list, are there any other issues that we need to discuss?" Often, the person looked at the list and added one or two more things. Because they saw that I was paying attention. Difficult people are like you and me: they just want to be heard. What I often found was that the last thing the person mentioned was the real reason they were in my office in the first place. It was the reason for the issue.

Usually, the last thing they said was the hardest to say. This was often because of an unmet expectation: "I don't feel understood," "I'm questioning my profession," "I'm not sure this is the best place for me," "I'm really having a hard time with the students," "There are some things going on at home." Often, if I was patient enough to wait and let the person tell me their perspective, the solution appeared.

Once everything was written down, I started to look for themes. I grouped these different issues, and then I said, "Now, what would your life be like if we were able to solve each of these issues—if this whiteboard was cleared up and we were able to move forward without these issues?"

When someone else seeks to find a solution to our problems, it can be off-putting. It can be a little surprising. What would life be like if all the issues were magically resolved? That's when they start to describe the solution: "I would feel valued again," "I would have more responsibility," "I would feel like I have a voice in the school," "I would feel like the students and parents respected me," "I would enjoy coming to work every day."

And that's it. That was the whole meeting. Often, positioning the meeting this way with someone who was giving me a hard time changed the dynamic, because I was truly trying to serve them. Even if the conversation was leading to them leaving. In many cases, approaching it this way made their long-term intention clear. Were they planning to stay? Clarifying those expectations, identifying the problems, clarifying the goal, and then working on the one step to move things forward changed everything.

If you apply the techniques I share in this chapter, you will find that difficult people start to show up less and less. Because the real change happens within yourself. And these strategies become second nature. Often, when you deal with difficult people directly from day one, they change their response toward you.

I'll close the chapter with this final story. As a first-year class-room teacher, I had a particularly difficult student. On the first day of school, while I was going over the classroom rules, she stood up in front of everyone in the class and announced, "This sucks! I'm out of here," and she walked out of the classroom. I later told my school administrator that I was flabbergasted, and her response floored me. "An effective teacher is never flabbergasted." I learned over the years that effective teachers expect to have difficult students from time to time. Instead of letting students surprise them, they learn strategies for dealing with someone who begins to present a problem, preventing the problem from growing larger.

After I learned a few of these strategies for dealing with difficult students, my second year of teaching was so much better. On the first day of school, while all of the students were waiting to receive a handshake and enter the classroom, one student burst out of line, saying, "Lines are for losers."

I calmly responded by shaking his hand, learning his name, and politely asking him to rejoin the back of the line. That one interaction won him over for the entire year. And as other teachers complained about his behavior in their class, I couldn't relate. I had learned a strategy that worked.

That's what you now have—a strategy for dealing with the difficult people in your life. So review this chapter and implement these techniques. Because even the most difficult people in your life are still your people.

Ideas to Consider

- Critics are never satisfied, but not all difficult people are critics.
- You decide on the volume level of your critics.
- What we dislike in ourselves we disdain in others.
- Your success will attract haters.

Actions to Take

- Be the first to make a move toward reconciliation.
- Recognize that family members may not always be your strongest supporters.
- Rearrange your office to make it conducive for handling disputes.

CHAPTER 10

Your Future Self

How to Be Who You Want to Be

I recently overheard the following conversation at a grocery store, between two employees. One lady said to the other, "What time do you get off?"

"Thirteen minutes," she said. "What about you?"

"I get off in thirteen minutes too."

"Well, what are you going to do?"

"I am going to stand here for thirteen minutes."

Up until this point, we've focused on relationships with other people. But there's one person we haven't talked about yet. It's the person you see every time you look in the mirror. Yourself.

At the grocery store, it took everything in me not to walk up to these ladies and say something. I wanted to explain how they were hurting more than the company. They were stealing from themselves. They were choosing the lesser life. Deciding to settle. But it wasn't my battle to fight. Instead as I drove away, I began to think about the areas in my life where I was just waiting out the clock. Where in my life was I counting down toward the weekend?

119

Where was I deciding to ignore a difficult issue instead of handling it like a grown-up? And that's exactly what this chapter is going to focus on.

Every day, you get to choose who you want to be. You get to choose how you want to show up. And in every situation, you can either add, subtract, or keep it the same. You can make things better, you can make things worse, or you can maintain the status quo. And if we're really honest, if you pay attention, I'm sure you'll see opportunities for improvement everywhere you look.

But often we are okay with just getting by. Doing just what's expected of us and maybe a little less. I call a person who adopts this approach a sustainer. And this is often the way we treat our life and work. Always running a little late but not too late. Finishing the project on time but not early. Just sustaining the normal.

But if you want to make a difference and lead a life you love, it's going to take more. It's going to take expectation plus. In Louisiana, they call this "lagniappe," just a little something extra. It's part of Southern hospitality, adding something special that was unexpected. It's what makes people feel awesome.

Well, what if you were to live the lagniappe life, doing a little something extra for people you work with, going the extra mile for people, noticing ways to improve your environment and taking initiative to make it happen?

You recognize gaps and make it your mission to close them. You're a problem solver, and you take initiative even when no one is watching. This is the life of a supplementer. They add to the situation, improving it for all around.

And finally, you can choose to be a subtractor. To make a situation worse. To take away from the list of expectations. To show up late, leave early, and not do everything that's expected. To frustrate others because you're not carrying your weight. And unfortunately, often it can seem that subtractors are the norm. As financial coach

Dave Ramsey says, "An employee is someone who comes in late, leaves early, and steals while they are here."[1]

So you have a choice, my friend. You get to decide who you want to be. When you think about your work, do you want to be a subtractor, somebody who makes the situation worse for other people, somebody who takes all they can get and leaves none for others, somebody who does less than what's expected?

Or do you want to be a sustainer, doing just enough to not get in trouble, just enough to fly under the radar without anyone noticing?

I challenge you to supplement, to make situations better, to add a little something extra, to be the one to take initiative, to show up for your people. The change that's required comes down to a decision between you and the person in the mirror.

That's the real decision this book is all about: Are you willing to level up your life? Will you start with your people? If so, you may be wondering what it takes to become a supplementer. It requires a clear vision, openness to feedback, and the patience to grow.

Develop a Clear Vision

Have you ever said to yourself, "Next year will be my best year"? And then, before you know it, another year rolls by and not much has changed. Personal development guru Jim Rohn was once advising a group of the world's leading CEOs. They asked him, "Jim, what will the next decade be like?" He answered in his characteristic way. "Well, gentlemen, I've had the opportunity to travel the world and speak with thousands of leaders over the last several decades. And I can tell you with absolute certainty that the next decade . . . will be

---

1   Dave Ramsey, *EntreLeadership: 20 Years of Practical Business Wisdom from the Trenches* (Nashville: Howard, 2011), 3.

pretty much the same as this one."[2] Don't you just love that? Next year will look about the same as this one, and maybe even a little worse, if you do not take the time to plan and reflect. My friend and mentor Dan Miller often says, "The best way to predict your future is to create it."[3] We need to be intentional about where we are going, if we ever hope to arrive at a destination worthy of our dreams.

Take a Look at the Map

As you look toward your future self, who you are becoming, view the stages you walk through as part of your "life map." At the time of this writing, my middle child, Emmaline, is only five years old. Statistically, she'll have a wedding in fifteen to twenty-five years. If the average wedding right now costs thirty thousand dollars, that means I need to save about fifteen hundred dollars per year in order to pay for a pretty awesome wedding. Don't be shocked at the cost of a wedding, like a subtractor or a sustainer would be. Instead look toward anticipated future events as part of your life map and prepare for these predictable destinations. After all, they are on the map!

The future is far enough away that you have time to change it, but it approaches quickly enough that you need to make the most of every opportunity. As you envision your future self, imagine who you will be ten years from now. Ten years is enough time to make major changes and achieve almost anything you desire. It is long enough to

- Go back to school, get trained in a new industry, and land the job of your dreams

2   Jim Rohn, "How to Take Charge of Your Life," YouTube (June 21, 2017), www.youtube.com/watch?v=DGIjuVbGP_A.

3   Dan Miller, *48 Days to the Work You Love: An Interactive Study* (Nashville: B&H Publishing Group, 2005), 29.

- Get the counseling you need to finally deal with that family situation and move forward
- Develop a good exercise and nutrition regimen and become the healthiest version of you
- Accomplish world-class, crazy dreams such as starting and selling a company, winning an award in your industry, and finally getting your finances together

As you look toward that future, consider how implementing a few daily habits would set you up for success ten years from now. Here's a three-step process I call Future Pacing.

1. Write down a specific goal you would like to achieve ten years from now.
2. Research the knowledge, connections, and costs involved in achieving that goal.
3. Establish one daily habit or routine to help make that goal a reality.

If you keep acting like you always have, you'll keep getting what you've always gotten. You are in control of more than you think. You control when you wake up, what you listen to, what you read, what you eat, and when you exercise. Habits happen one day at a time. One year from now, you'll wish that you had started today.

Receiving Feedback

Become self-aware enough to know your weaknesses. The mark of character will be not how good you are but how much you are willing to improve. A key part of this improvement process is asking for and listening to feedback from others. Yes, we need to choose who we allow to speak into our lives. But trusted friends and mentors must know that we are open and available to receiving their feed-back. Feedback, when it's negative, can put us on the defensive. But what if you could view feedback as an opportunity to grow, a chance to identify a few areas for improvement? Making a change, no matter how small or seemingly insignificant, is never easy.

As I realized about myself when I completed the 360 Assessment, you too may have a few blind spots that are worth addressing. And no one feels safe enough to tell you about them. It's hard to give feedback that may hurt someone's feelings or cause them to lash out. Sometimes it's just easier to keep our mouth shut than to tell a friend about their flaws. But if you dig deep, you'll see that you've already received the feedback you need to become the best version of yourself. The truth is hidden in a formal review at your work-place. Or in a sly comment, a snarky remark, or an ongoing joke. "She's never on time." "He always has to have the last word." "She can't take criticism." "He always sleeps in." Although these com-ments may hurt, consider whether there is any truth to them. Don't shoot the messenger before you consider the message; it might just be what you need to hear. Even inside a joke there is often a seed of truth.

I would love to tell you I have a thick skin and that negative comments just bounce right off. But negative feedback can eat at me for days, weeks, or even months. I take what was said, and I multiply it by a million.

As an example, once I spoke at a friend's conference. It was an awesome speech, and afterward I had people lined up for hours, asking for my feedback and advice.

A few weeks after the conference, my friend called, and we spoke for more than thirty minutes about our lives and our businesses. He told me he was reviewing the feedback forms from the conference. There were hundreds of positive comments. But one feedback card said I used the word *okay* too much in my keynote speech.

My dear friend used all sorts of disclaimers and said it in the kindest way. It was his one suggestion for improving my delivery of a life-changing message. One comment. "Try to use the word *okay* a little less. When you say *okay* too much, it can be a little annoying."

That conversation stuck with me for months. Yes, months. Every time I thought of this friend, I replayed that comment. But it did help me improve my communication. The next time I spoke at a conference, I eliminated that negative habit.

If you have a tough time receiving negative feedback, I empathize with you. It's something we all struggle with. But that feedback made me a better speaker. And the long-term improvement is worth the temporary pain. Okay? (LOL)

Patience to Grow

You do not become skilled overnight. Life is not *American Idol*. Growth takes years of hard work and dedication. But most of all, it takes honesty. You need to be real with yourself. "Here is an area of struggle. Here is where I need some help." The only way to get better is facing reality and moving forward with a plan. And plans take time. You will make mistakes. Success will take longer than you want. But instead of aiming for perfection tomorrow, take the advice of entrepreneur and bestselling author Donald Miller and peak at sixty-five. He explains, "Peaking at 65 means doing excellent work over the long haul."[4] Being successful takes discipline, focus, feedback, and self-reflection over a long period of time.

---

4   Donald Miller, "The Failure of Twenty-Something Thinking and Why You Should Peak at 65," Storyline (December 4, 2012), *http://storylineblog.com/2012/12/04/why-you-should-peak-at-65/*.

Becoming a Mentor

One of my life's greatest joys is investing in other people, particularly younger men with leadership potential. You too may be passionate about helping someone reach their next level of success. Mentoring relationships have been rewarding both for me and for my mentees. Consider who you might be able to reach out to and mentor. Often, a mentee is nervous and doesn't know how to ask but could really benefit from a relationship with you. Start with a few informal conversations to see if they seek out and listen to your advice. Then take them out to lunch and get to know them. If it seems like a good fit and you believe that you can offer some value, set a regular time to meet. So much of what I've been able to experience in my life is because of the investment of a mentor. I'm grateful for the men and women who saw potential in me and took the risk to reach out. Supplementers know that it's our duty (and privilege) to give back and help others grow.

Daily Gratitude

The danger of setting big goals is resenting the present. What I have now isn't good enough compared with my future goals. Expressing gratitude for our progress, no matter how small or slow, makes the difference. Being grateful for what we have, who we know, and what we are in this moment is not giving up; it is building up. Gratitude helps us recognize that we are farther along than we think, we are more than we feel, we have more than we remember. And that far-off goal is closer than it appears to be. Gratitude in the present provides encouragement, momentum, and the drive to move forward into the future. Be grateful for where you are today as you look toward tomorrow. Be present right now. See the joy in the journey.

The Story You Tell Yourself

Our beliefs about ourselves impact what we see. As psychiatrist Curt Thompson explained, "Each of us lives within a story we believe we occupy."[5] The preacher you listen to the most is you. What are you saying to yourself? What is the story you are telling yourself? How have you woven all of these events together to create a narrative arc? At the end of today, you can find all of the ways someone has been unkind or neglected you. You can also find all the ways you have been treated well. You create the pattern. You recognize the common thread. We are pattern-making people. Be careful which story you are telling yourself. What if you are underestimating your capabilities?

Every so often, usually in the middle of a really busy day, I catch a glimpse of my face in the mirror. I spend most of my day in my own head, thinking about my goals and priorities, trying to get work done and do the best I can. But then, out of the corner of my eye, I notice myself in the mirror. I've learned to use these mirror moments as an opportunity for a quick pep talk. There I am. This is me. With all the possibilities and limitations I've been gifted. Yes, I have limitations. I'm limited by my physical body, connections, energy level, finances, and relationships. There is only so much I can accomplish with the time I have. But I can choose what I do within these limitations. I have agency over much of my day. And there is power in limitation. So I ask, "If this is all I have, how can I best use these resources? How can I take what I've been gifted and use

---

5   Curt Thompson, *The Soul of Shame* (Downers Grove: InterVarsity Press, 2015), 12.

it for maximum effect? How can I leverage my resources to impact the greatest number of people?"

Three Steps to Level Up Your Life

You're still with me. You've decided to be a supplementer and become the best version of your future self. You want to level up your life? Well, here are three steps to help you do just that.

Take 100 Percent Responsibility

The first step is acknowledging the truth. It's dropping the blame you're holding against other people and taking responsibility for your results. You are where you are because of your choices. It might not be 100 percent your fault, but you can take 100 percent responsibility. You can move forward in freedom and stop blaming external circumstances and other people. You can decide today to take ownership of your life. Make the decision to let go of the blame and say, "If it is to be, it is up to me."

Listen, I have waited. I've been in frustrating situations. I've had miserable jobs. I've worked with difficult people. Yet no matter what, I still had control over my facial expression, my body language, and my tone. I had to decide to check out or step up. And you get to decide this too. If you're frustrated with your current job, family situation, money, fitness, whatever it is, claim agency over your life.

You might have people in your life you want to change. I could name people right now who I wish were different in some way or another. I've expressed my frustration out loud to my wife. "If only he would let me run his life for one week, things would change. I would quit that job for him, I would apply to those jobs for him, I would fix his outfit, work on his exercise plan, and finally make the hard decisions he's been putting off his whole life." But ultimately,

I'm not in charge of the lives of my people. Not even my kids, my spouse, or my best friends. The only person I have direct agency over is myself. That's where change must begin. I can change me, and others will decide what they see.

I can start walking around the block every day after dinner. I can say no to an after-dinner bowl of ice cream. I can start reading inspirational books. If the people in my life want to join me, that's up to them. Stop looking toward other people and instead implement the change you want to see in your own life.

Ask for Help

The second step in leveling up your life is asking for help. No one succeeds on their own. Everyone has a team. Entrepreneurial coach Chris Ducker says, "There's a team of people behind almost every successful person I've met."[6] In my coaching practice, when a client is particularly stuck, I often recommend they get help from an outside person. There are usually two responses. Either they're willing to get that assistance, or they try to do it on their own. When they choose to go it alone, they are usually dealing with the same issues months later. When they decide to ask for help, forward momentum helps them reach new opportunities for growth.

We need to reach out beyond ourselves to get external help. When you're inside the bottle, it's impossible to read the label. That's why we need other people. Find a mentor, a mastermind, and a team. Allow these people to speak into your life and be honest with you.

Take Action on What You're Learning

The final step in leveling up your life is to take action on the knowledge you are acquiring. Too often, we use learning as another form

---

6   Chris Ducker, "3 Software Platforms to Help Manage Your Virtual Business," www.chrisducker.com/software-manage-virtual-business/.

of procrastination. We attend another conference, listen to another audiobook, download another podcast, only to keep tickling our ears and feeding our brains but never moving our feet and using our hands. Take action on what you are learning. Unapplied knowledge has no value. Instead take action on what you already know. Much of our learning is just procrastination.

- With so much emphasis on schooling, good grades, and studying hard, a better question is, what are you studying for?
- What action are you taking that is leading to a particular outcome or event? What is the purpose of all this learning?

The question now is, where do you start? As they say, the best time to plant a tree was twenty years ago, but the second-best time is today. And that's what you have. You have the gift of today. You can take action right now. You don't have to get it perfect; you just have to get it going.[7] Following, as in the other chapters, you'll see a list of ideas to consider and actions to take. Choose one of these actions and move forward on it today. The only way for things to change is for you to be willing to change. Your future self will thank you.

Ideas to Consider

- Our internal voices are the ones we listen to more than any other. Use your future self to define who you are and who you want to become ("Dear younger me, . . .").
- We are either subtractors (taking away value and wasting time), sustainers (holding the status quo), or supplementers

---

7   This is a saying I picked up from Ryan Levesque.

(adding value and spending time wisely). We choose which we will be in any given moment.

- We are at our best when we stop trying to control everything around us and focus on what we ultimately can control: ourselves.

Actions to Take

- Take a personal inventory in order to understand your capabilities and take responsibility for your actions.
- Identify which you are: a subtractor, a sustainer, or a supplementer.
- Ask yourself the following questions and write down the answers. "Where in my life do I need to relinquish control?"
- "What areas of myself might I change to improve my situation?"
- "What adjustments do I need to make to move more in step with who I am?"
- "What are two or three things my future self might say to me today? And how might this change how I am living and working now?"

PART 2

PURPOSE

 Uncovering Your People-First Mission

Just imagine waking up every day excited to get to work! Clarifying your purpose will lead you to this level of enthusiasm. When we know who we serve and how we help, we live with the confidence that we are on the right track and making the most out of every opportunity.

Do you know your purpose? Can you summarize it in just a few sentences? That's the promise of this section. Over the next three chapters, you will follow a proven process to discover your sweet spot.

It's time to talk about your purpose. After reading this section, you'll be able to answer that most annoying party question "So what do you do?" with confidence. Let's explore the path to helping your dream customer and creating your all-important purpose statement.

CHAPTER 11

Show Up and Serve

'll never forget the voicemail I received from my friend Scott on a Thursday afternoon. "Hey, Brian, unfortunately, I'm going to have to cancel our lunch tomorrow. I'll be in a recording session with Larry." It was the greatest rejection voicemail I've ever received. But for you to understand that, you would need to know a little bit about Scott, Larry, and what they were recording.

Scott's dream was to be a composer. More specific, he wanted to write the music you hear in movies. He had a dream to create epic film scores, writing and recording every note that plays during the battle scene of a blockbuster movie. He had the right gear and training but no way to get his foot in the door of this highly competitive industry.

Julie and I met Scott when we moved to San Diego. We were living in a tiny apartment near the beach, and Scott was our next-door neighbor. I think he sold insurance at the time. Then one day, I saw him carrying an enormous keyboard from his tiny hatchback car up the two flights of stairs to his apartment. I held the door open for him and caught a glimpse of his dream. His tiny one-bedroom apartment had been transformed into a state-of-the-art recording studio. He had all of the equipment to create the music for an Academy Award–winning film. But there was only one problem. Scott couldn't get anyone to listen to his demo. He'd recorded sample music showing what he could do, but no one was interested in giving him a chance. He put his dream off to the side, feigning contentment and calling music production a hobby.

It's easy to do. When our dream fails to materialize, it can be tempting to minimize it and call it a side project, just something we'll get around to someday. But after seeing the inside of his apartment, I knew the truth. Scott's dream was much bigger than selling insurance.

And maybe that's where you are right now. Maybe there is a dream you've had for a while, longer than you can remember, that you've downgraded from a daily obsession to a weekend hobby shelved away in a guest room closet or somewhere in the attic.

After hearing a sample of his compositions, I just couldn't let it go. Scott had talent. Over time, we began to hang out. Every few weeks, we'd go see a movie, and afterward all he could talk about was the movie's score.

And yet each morning, I'd see lifeless Scott, briefcase in hand, heading off to fight the San Diego traffic, trudging to a job he despised.

Julie and I moved a few towns away and lost touch with Scott. A few years passed. Then one night, I just happened to run into Scott at a gas station. We made plans to grab lunch on a Friday. There was a spark in his eye that I hadn't seen before. A few days later, I received the voicemail canceling our plans. As it turns out, Scott hadn't given up on his dream. To his credit, he had tried all of the traditional ways to get his foot in the door as a composer. He submitted his demo CD, he applied for independent productions, he worked for free just to build his resume, but nothing was leading to his dream.

He was browsing the website of Larry, a well-known film composer living in San Diego, when he noticed a spelling error. Then, in the next paragraph, another one. Scott began to make a list of all the spelling and grammatical errors on the website. Now, granted, as a classically trained composer, Scott paid meticulous attention to details, so he felt compelled to do something. From a heart of service, he drafted a short email to the contact link on Larry's website, outlining the errors and suggested fixes.

And that's where the story usually ends. Except things didn't end there for Scott. They were just beginning. Less than five minutes after Scott sent that email, his phone rang. It was Larry.

"Scott. Thanks for your advice on my website. I forwarded your email to my team to fix the site. By the way, your website mentioned you have experience with this new composing software program. I'm wondering if you could come by the studio and give me a tutorial."

Scott was speechless. All he could muster in response was, "Sounds great. See you soon." Thirty minutes later, he was standing in the composer's oceanfront studio, helping him learn the latest version of a software program that Scott knew inside and out.

Over the next few years, this relationship blossomed. Scott is now a full-time composer in Hollywood, living his dream and improving moviegoers' experiences across the world. You see, all of the traditional means of getting noticed didn't work for Scott. None of them led him closer to his dream. The key that finally opened the locked door to his profitable purpose was a heart of service. To get ahead, you need to show up and serve.

Showing up and serving is the best way to get the raise you've been longing for, increase sales of your existing product, or finally land your dream job. Get your foot in the door by offering to hold the door open for other people. This is the secret key to building relationships with influencers.

Living your purpose starts with showing up and serving. It's not about you. It's about helping them.

Imagine if you could look at your life and work on being on a mission for people. Imagine if your goal were to make their day and to help them win the day. Not only would your life be fulfilling, but you would be rewarded for your efforts. Your company would grow, you would get promoted, and you would feel a sense of fulfillment far beyond anything you've experienced before.

Be on a mission for people. When you are on a mission, even the most mundane task has a weighty level of importance. Delivering a meal to a family who just had a baby, pumping gas for an ambulance, or setting up an internet connection so a dying family member can make a video call to their loved ones one last time. Your contribution is monumental when the stakes are high.

Don't have any connections? Show up and serve.

Tired of the job hunt? Show up and serve.

Can't get anyone on the phone? Show up and serve.

Showing up and serving will open up new opportunities and make a massive difference in your life and in the lives of others.

Let's take a look at Mike's story. Mike is a great marketer and copywriter, but he wasn't always that way. He started out as a musician and worship leader for his church. His day job, as the head of marketing for an educational company, was slowly killing him. Something needed to change if he was ever going to live a life he loved. He signed up for Michael Hyatt's Platform Conference, where he met an expert copywriter named Ray Edwards.

Ray, a legend in his industry, was making a transition from client work to coaching and teaching. Mike recognized the opportunity for mentorship, and he went all in. He invested in Ray's most expensive mentorship program. He followed Ray's teaching and became his best student. He did everything he could to serve Ray: helping at his events, promoting his programs, and assisting Ray's clients. And Ray noticed. Before too long, Ray was using Mike as a case study. Mike's success was Ray's success. Once Mike had proven his value to Ray, a consistent stream of clients followed.

Ray began to refer hundreds of thousands of dollars' worth of client work to Mike. Ray was the Big Domino for Mike. Mike has now become one of the best-known copywriters in his industry. And it all started with Ray.

Influential people like Ray maintain a tight-knit circle. They are used to people asking for things from them all the time, so they've learned to be a little guarded. The key in reaching influencers is to build a relationship with them. It's simply a matter of paying your dues. Influential people have a lot to lose if you waste their time, so they are naturally more skeptical. But once you have shown value for one influential person, they introduce you to their network, and other opportunities begin to fall in your lap.

Consider Their Goals

Everyone has a goal. If you're trying to build a relationship with an influencer at a conference, figure out her goal for the conference. If she's an author, she likely wants to make a connection with her readers, sell more books, deliver a smooth presentation, and collect names for her email list. Each one of these goals has several volunteer opportunities. Showing up and serving is as easy as getting there a little early and offering to help set up the book table or staying a little later and offering to carry books back to the car. It's amazing the difference a helping hand can make when offered at the right time.

The same is true with companies you might want to work for. Consider their goals. Most companies publish their goals in their annual report, on their website, or on their social media accounts. If the goal is to become the industry leader in the region, consider ways you might help them reach their goal. Maybe it's introducing a new contact, recommending a vendor, volunteering at a trade show, or serving alongside them in their community outreach efforts.

Break through the Gatekeepers

For months, I tried to get the attention of a well-known singer-songwriter. I knew that his unique approach to songwriting was well respected and that others would benefit from learning his process. But it was nearly impossible to get through to him to pitch the idea. I had tried everything. I wrote emails, posted messages on social media, and attended two concerts, hoping to have a conversation. But nothing was working.

Then one day, I noticed an email newsletter announcing that he would be teaching a songwriting workshop at an arts festival just two hours away. Even though I wasn't interested in the majority of the festival, I knew this could be my opportunity to finally meet him and pitch the idea of publishing an online course with my company.

I got to the festival early, went directly to his session, and sat in the front row, waiting for my opportunity to introduce myself. At the right moment, I walked up, reached out my hand, and said, "Hi, I'm Brian. I produce online video courses, and I think you could have an amazing online songwriting course."

His response was simple but profound. He shook my hand and said, "I've been looking for someone like you."

All it took was one handshake and a clear pitch. And you can do the same. That's the best way to approach them. To meet in person and say, "It looks like you're trying to do X, and I have a way to help you."

Everyone Needs Help

Think about the most famous person in your field. Maybe it's a well-known musician or athlete. Perhaps it's a famous speaker or author. Maybe it's a key business leader or an influential politician.

No one succeeds completely on their own. Everyone has a team. The key is remembering that they need help, anticipating their needs, and being willing to be at the right place at the right time.

The more well-known the person, the higher their guard will be. Everyone wants something from them. That's why you need to approach them with a posture of service. Showing up and serving, saying, "I'm here to help." That's really all you need to say. "I am here to help. Put me to work." Not taking no for an answer, and offering a specific solution, will help you get your foot in the door. Be willing to do what most people won't.

Figuring out your purpose starts with finding out how you can help your people.

My Favorite Question to Ask

When I meet people at a conference or professional meetup, my favorite question to ask is, "What are you working through?" It's a very approachable question. It sounds kind of like you're asking, "How are you?" but really you're asking them where they're struggling. So ask your people, "What are you working through?" Often, they'll tell you and you'll find a way to help them.

Dave helps companies fund construction projects by offering low-interest loans. Dave can call his list of thirty prospects in the construction niche that are within a hundred miles from Charlotte, and he can introduce himself and ask them about their current challenges. "It's Dave. I work with X corporation and I'm wondering, what are you working through?"

Dave positions himself as the one person who cares. Imagine you are Dave and you make such a call. If they say, "Oh, you know, thanks for asking. We're actually trying to hire a new secretary." You simply say, "Okay, thanks for letting me know. Let me think about how I can help with that," and then you hang up the phone.

You post on your Facebook page, "X construction company in X town is looking for a new secretary. Anybody know anybody?" and tag them. Then you reach back out to your contact with a screenshot and a few introductions through email.

Think about what that would mean for the company. You are the person who went above and beyond to help them with their goals. Your purpose is to help make their dreams come true. It's not to sell construction loans. But when they need a construction loan, you are the first person they're thinking about.

After attending a concert, church service, or industry conference, make a list of what you observed. What went well? What could be improved? Then send a note to the organizer, telling them, "These are three things you guys did well. Here is one area for improvement where I would be willing to step in. I could provide my service in this one key area, which will help you reach your goal [increase attendance, better serve your members, increase revenue, make your life easier]." Listen to people's needs and lead with that. Offering a solution often leads to connections, business, and opportunity.

What's Obvious to You Is Magic to Other People

A few weeks ago at our church, one of the singers accidentally lowered her microphone toward the monitor. It made a loud feedback sound. The screech was so loud that it really distracted from the service. As somebody who was in a band for several years and understands audio production, I realized that our church didn't have a feedback eliminator. It's a simple piece of equipment that costs just a few hundred dollars. It ensures that this kind of screeching feedback never happens again. It was obvious to me that our church needed one. I just opened up the Amazon app on my phone and ordered it. By the next Sunday, they had it installed, and we haven't had any feedback problems since.

In the same way, you have your own unique experience. You recognize certain things because of the countless hours you've been a pro in your industry. You've learned so much the hard way. That knowledge is valuable to other people. When you show up, serve, and provide value, often what you think is simple and easy can be complicated and overwhelming for others.

You spend your entire life learning to become who you are. Your knowledge is so valuable to people who are just starting out. But what often happens is that we discredit our experience. We don't believe that our knowledge is valuable, so we think there's no reason somebody would want to hire us or work with us or allow us to show up and serve. But the opposite is true. What's obvious to you is magic to other people.

I don't consider myself much of a tech guru, but compared with my seventy-plus-year-old father-in-law, you would think I invented the computer. I don't consider myself much of an athlete, but compared with somebody who's never run a 5K, I might as well be an Olympic star. I really try my best to be an engaged dad, but to someone expecting his first child, I have a wealth of knowledge to share about raising kids. And the same is true for you. Who you are now is invaluable to those who have not yet experienced what you've gone through.

People Support What They Help Create

When I advise a coaching client, help an influencer create a course, or help an author plan their book launch, I'm invested in the outcome of that project. That person's success reflects on me. When you show up and serve, when you help your mentor create a new program, have a great experience, or market a product, they are invested in the outcome. They are invested in you.

One day, John was visiting the blog of bestselling author and business leader Michael Hyatt when he noticed that a lot of people had questions about Michael's "Get Noticed" WordPress theme. John started doing "Get Noticed" theme installations and consulting. He helped other people have success with Michael's program. He did this on his own, and he became the go-to guy to help with the "Get Noticed" theme. And Michael took notice. When people had questions about the theme, Michael began referring them to John and his company. Over time, that relationship blossomed, and eventually Michael hired John to be his full-time director at Platform University, one of Michael's premier brands. It all started when John paid attention, showed up, and served.

My Big Domino was career coach and *New York Times* bestselling author Dan Miller. I was one of his avid podcast listeners and readers. My long-term goal was to partner with Dan to help him scale his online business, grow his email list, and launch online courses. But that wasn't where I started. Instead I showed up and served. I attended one of his conferences and acted like a volunteer even though I paid to go there. I offered to pick up attendees' lunch plates, gave directions to the bathroom, and handed out water bottles. I did anything I could do to serve Dan's people and therefore serve Dan. This was being strategic, not manipulative; people can see through tactics when they don't come from a heart of service. I really respected Dan, and I wanted to help him serve his audience well. Dan didn't hire me right away. But I did make an impression.

Next, I attended a conference put on by one of Dan's close friends, Kent Julian. I paid for the conference registration and hotel room, but I showed up to serve as if I were a volunteer. I helped people get checked in. I offered directions at lunch. Most important, I paid attention to Kent's goals.

At this conference, Kent mentioned that an online introductory video was a great asset to help you stand out in a crowded marketplace. None of the conference attendees, who were all hoping to be professional speakers, had one. And this was my opportunity.

I knew how to make videos. I emailed Kent and offered to produce these videos at his next conference for free. That's right, I
would travel to Atlanta, bring my equipment, film videos for every
attendee, edit and share the videos with them—all for free. Kent
was blown away. Plus, it was a great opportunity for me to practice
my skills with real people, gain testimonials for my work, and build
a relationship with my Big Domino.

The Triangle of Credibility

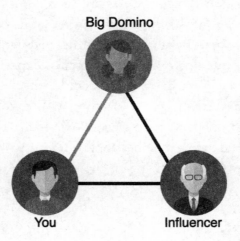

This is what I call the Triangle of Credibility. The best way
to work with your Big Domino is to have another influencer they
know and trust vouch for you. High-level people validate a relationship before they move forward. If they've been around awhile, they
are smart enough to avoid being burned. Reputation and portfolio
are two key tools to prevent disappointment and frustration. Before
saying yes to you, they often check in with their friends.

The conference went well, and after I received a glowing testimonial from Kent, I asked if he would reach out to Dan for me. He

was happy to do it. Dan allowed me to attend his next conference for free, stay at his house, and even have lunch with him after the conference was over. I drove to Nashville with my video equipment, showed up, and served his people, filming forty introductory videos over the course of two days. I edited all of the videos and posted them within a week of the conference. I was committed to overdelivering for Dan and his people.

And then came the email that changed it all for me. Dan invited me to speak at his next conference. Bingo! All of that showing up and serving had finally led to the opportunity I was working for.

At the next conference, Dan introduced me to his audience. "We do business with people we know, like, and trust. And that describes Brian. This is the third conference that he's attended, and he's here to serve you. Because he is serving you, he is serving me. He's helping me provide a better conference experience for you. And that's why we do business with Brian."

I went on to speak at Dan's Coaching with Excellence conference five more times and have since partnered with Dan in the creation of his paid online membership community, 48 Days Eagles.

Here are some ideas to help you show up and serve.

- Volunteer
- Help with sales
- Introduce new leads
- Share new vendors
- Offer tech tips
- Optimize existing platform
- Make a connection
- Network
- Proactively solve challenges
- Anticipate needs
- Make phone calls
- Help set up or clean up

- Promote the work of others
- Be a case study

In other words, you start with your people by showing up for them.

You cannot do it all. But there is a lot you can do. You can show up for people. In the major (and minor) relationships in your life, you already know what you need to do.

You know your grandmother needs new batteries for her TV remote, so you buy the batteries on Amazon while at her house, and then you install the batteries for her the next time you are there. You tell a work colleague that you'll email them the report. You schedule a reminder. You make sure it gets done. You become someone who shows up for people. Someone who does the things he said he would do.

As we finish the first chapter in this section on purpose, your purpose is now clear. You're on a mission for people. When you show up and serve, and add value to those around you, opportunities will begin to present themselves. You'll develop a reputation in your industry. And people will begin to rely on you. This is not complicated. All you need to do is show up and serve. That's the difference when you start with your people.

Ideas to Consider

- Show up and serve people right where you are, right now, and your mission will follow.
- Figuring out your purpose starts with finding out how you can help your people.
- Offering a solution to someone's problem often leads to connections, business, and opportunity.
- The knowledge you have gained from your experiences is valuable to people who are just starting out. The things

you think are simple and easy can be complicated and overwhelming for others.

■ People will invest in you when you show up and serve.

Actions to Take

■ Research the goals of a company you would like to work for, and write down ways you can help them reach their goals.

■ Begin asking, "What are you working through?" in your interactions with others. Discover what they are struggling with and figure out how you can help.

■ Make a list of specific ways you can serve others in your life.

CHAPTER 12

Create Your Purpose Statement

I f you had seen me that sunny May morning, you would have thought I had it all together. Having started my business a year before, I had flown out to the beautiful San Clemente beach in California to do some vision casting. Walking along the beach with a California burrito in one hand, a fresh cup of cappuccino in the other, and my Moleskine journal in my back pocket, I was set to redefine the purpose of our company.

I had left my six-figure nonprofit CEO position a year earlier to start my own company, and I was really stuck. Starting and growing the school had been challenging, but getting my company off the ground felt impossible. I was in California to attend two masterminds, with the hope that across the span of one week I could figure everything out. There I was, in California, walking and vision casting, when my phone rang. It was my wife. I thought about not answering it, because we both knew why I was really in San Clemente. We were about to give up on this business.

I answered the phone, and I'll never forget what she said to me. "Have you checked our bank account?" She informed me that the cost of my trip had put us back into debt. At this point, we were coaches for Dave Ramsey's money management program called Financial Peace University. I had cut up my credit card about a year and a half before to show, "We are debt free! We're never going back." And yet here we were. It was only a few hundred dollars, but we knew it was the beginning of a train that we did not want to ride again. That phone call from Julie made me realize that our situation was more desperate than I thought.

The next day, I went to the mastermind at a beautiful hotel in downtown San Diego. I met all kinds of people I was acquainted with from an online business course I'd taken. They were all telling me about how great their businesses were. When I got to my hot seat session, I faked it. I wasn't ready. I talked about my services and packages and the different things that I was going to be offering. As that day ended, not one person hired me.

Discouraged, I canceled my plans that night and drove to the beach. I watched the sunset, head in hands. I didn't even call Julie that night. I was too discouraged to call her. I felt defeated.

I spent the whole week wandering—walking and running up and down the beach, holing myself up in coffee shops—trying to figure out what we were going to do with this thing I had created.

I was sitting in a Starbucks in Oceanside, California, when I got invited to a Facebook group composed of people attending the second mastermind who wanted to connect before Saturday. I had also signed up for a hot seat session and knew my goal was to get this thing figured out over the course of the week. But I had no idea what I was going to offer. What I'd tried in the other mastermind hadn't worked. I knew I needed another strategy.

Instead of thinking about what I was going to do, I started to get to know the other attendees. I clicked on each person's profile, read through their story, and looked at the questions they had asked. Scrolling through these profiles, I began to discover my who.

Prior to this, I was clear on my what and why, but now I was beginning to discover my who. My pitch at that mastermind had been about me. "This is what I'm going to do, look at my team, look at my services, look at my fancy website." No one connected to me, because I was not putting them first.

Discovering my who over the course of that week was profound. Now I know who I'm serving with my what and why.

I call her Sheryl. She is my customer avatar—an amalgamation of a few people—who I point to as my perfect client. I wrote out a narrative description of Sheryl.

> Sheryl has a message to share and an audience to serve. She is passionate about helping her readers experience growth in their life through her weekly blog, inspirational Instagram posts, and encouraging podcast interviews. She dreams about writing a book one day but is a little confused by the process. Although she has her own website, she's a little overwhelmed by the tech part. She wishes she had a business coach to encourage her in the challenges, help inspire her to keep moving forward, and answer her questions about strategy and technology.

A few days later at the mastermind, in front of a roomful of my ideal clients, I had another chance to pitch my business. But instead of talking about me and my company and my services and how great I was, I spoke about Sheryl.

As it turns out, there were four Sheryls in the room. Four people who connected with my what because they were my who.

I landed four clients that day. That was the day my business actually started. That was the day I stopped focusing on what I do and instead figured out who it is that I serve.

When we start with our who, we begin the journey toward our profitable purpose. We help our dream customer accomplish their goal. I've learned that what's obvious to you is magic to other people. I thought, *Oh, of course everybody knows how to do an Infusionsoft campaign; it's just math.* But I work with people who are allergic to math.

Two years later, I found myself back in San Clemente, walking the same path. I was there to attend a conference, host a meetup, and connect with friends in the industry. My business was rocking because I was focused on my who. Watching the surfers, I was thinking back to that awkward conversation on the phone with Julie when my phone vibrated. But this time it wasn't Julie. It was a notification from PayPal. A client's monthly retainer payment had just gone through. With gratitude I walked the beach that morning, reflecting on all I had learned. By starting with my people, I'd gained clarity for my business, confidence in my coaching services, and abundant finances to make a difference for the people who matter most.

That's possible for you too. To help you discover your who, I'd love to walk you through two exercises in the remainder of this chapter.

The first exercise will help you identify your profitable purpose. It's the 1 percent that makes 99 percent of the difference. It's where your work, demand, passion, and platform intersect.

The second exercise will help you create your Mirror Manifesto. This is a short statement you can review each morning to give you the clarity and confidence to face the day and serve your people.

Your Profitable Purpose

I have realized that a dream is not about starting something new. It's about rediscovering a great passion that was abandoned in favor of other people's expectations, a longing for security, and a desire to fit in. You likely already know your life's deepest purpose, but you may not be consciously aware of it. It is hidden somewhere deep inside you, buried by layers of family expectations, unplanned circumstances, and unintended consequences. It's time to mine the soil of your personal history to discover the acres of diamonds buried there. My friend Ben Arment explains, "Your dream is the outcome of a life lived up until this point, not a new beginning. You don't go after your dream. Your dream comes after you."[1]

In this section, I'll help you see the relationship between the work you do, the passion you live out, and the people you serve. As Angela Duckworth explains in her book *Grit*, "At its core, the idea of purpose is the idea that what we do matters to people other than ourselves."[2] Discovering your profitable purpose is like putting a puzzle together. Each piece adds to the whole, giving a fuller picture of who you are and what is possible. There are four pieces that make up your profitable purpose.

1. The first piece of the puzzle represents the work you do. It's the easiest place to start, because the work is tangible; there's a product or service for a specific customer. It's the actual work we do. You might answer phones or make sales calls. Maybe you assist clients or create new proposals. Maybe you are particularly skilled at writing, speaking, building, designing, or teaching.

work

2. The second piece of the puzzle of profitable purpose represents the demand for your work skills. Ask yourself, "Is anybody actually hiring for this type of work?" If so, you have the potential for a job. The work you do connects with the needs people have. Here's where things start to get interesting. Just because you are skilled at doing something doesn't mean that people want to pay

1   Ben Arment, *Dream Year* (New York: Penguin, 2014), 22.
2   Angela Duckworth, *Grit: The Power of Passion and Perseverance* (New York: Scribner, 2016), 145.

for it. Here are a few ways to determine market demand for the work you offer. You can see what people are hiring for

by going to job posting websites. You can view hiring trends and look at market forces in industry publications. Being aware of the demand for the work you offer can help you sharpen your skills in response to where your company or your industry is headed.

3. The third piece represents your passion. Ask yourself, "Do I enjoy the work I do? Is this pursuit something I want to sign my name to, build a brand on, and create my life around? Is

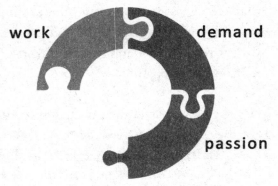

this something I'd still be eagerly talking about even if I wasn't getting paid?" Passion is what keeps you going when the going gets tough. When you're discouraged and want to give up, passion is what helps push you through. My favorite way to identify passion is the bookstore test. Imagine that you have an hour free at a bookstore. What section of the bookstore do you naturally go to? What topics are you interested in learning more about? What are you voracious about? What subjects are you constantly wanting to learn and grow in? This is your passion.

Now, here's where the exercise gets interesting. When work, demand, and passion overlap, you've discovered your sweet spot. But there's one more element you need in order to uncover your profitable purpose.

4. The way to move from your sweet spot to your profitable purpose is to add a fourth piece: reach. Your reach is a culmination of your email list, your social media following,

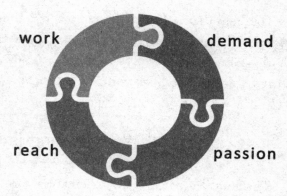

your relationships with influencers, and all of the connections you have in your industry. Your reach is how you connect to the right people. With the right reach, you can engage just the right people online who need your services and are willing to pay a premium to work with you. The internet enables us to serve anyone across the globe with our products and services. All of us can reach our ideal market. But the way in which you do that can vary depending on your experience, your level of industry expertise, and what kind of market you're in.

With a connected network and a reputation, you'll achieve the reach you need to help you live at your full potential. Sure, you have to have skills to do the work. You could get a job based on market

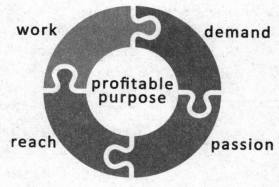

demand. You could pursue a career with passion. But reach is the final piece of the puzzle that leads to your profitable purpose.

Notice that your profitable purpose starts with your people. The work you do is for people. Market demand is about meeting the needs of people. Passion is about who you want to serve and how you help them. And of course reach is the connection you have to the right people to help your business grow. When you put together these four pieces, you're ready to live out your profitable purpose. It's how you establish yourself as a people-first leader.

What If Something Is Missing?

The four pieces combine to create a carefully balanced model for success. If one of those key components is missing, it could lead to boredom, failure, or poverty. Without work, there is no traction. There's no income to pay the bills. Without demand for your products or services, no one is hiring you. It's just a hobby. Without passion, work becomes monotonous. You'll jump from job to job, looking for the next pay raise, but you'll eventually burn out because there is no joy in the work. Without reach, you won't be able to scale up your business to create the greatest impact in your community and industry.

Need a few clues to figure out these puzzle pieces? Spend some time dwelling on the following questions. They will help you discover your profitable purpose.

What do you daydream about?

What do you love learning about?

What would you do if money were not an issue?

Clarifying Your Purpose

Think big about who you are and
what you offer the world.

—MICHAEL PORT[3]

---

3   Michael Port, *Book Yourself Solid: The Fastest, Easiest, and Most Reliable System for Getting More Clients Than You Can Handle Even if You Hate Marketing and Selling* (Hoboken:

You've seen the puzzle put together and understand why each piece is important, but you may not be sure how to assemble the pieces of your life. Here are a few actions you can take to begin the process.

Ask Your Friends on Social Media
Post the following status on Facebook.

> Weird question alert: I'm working to find clarity in my life and in my career. Here's a question for you, and it would mean the world to me if you'd answer as a comment below: What am I good at? Thank you so much.

Your friends will give you feedback, and the exercise will be both humbling and empowering.

Change Up Your Environment
One way to clarify your purpose is to go away for a bit and consider your life from a distance. This might mean going to the mountains or spending a weekend at the beach. Change up your environment to clarify your purpose. It might be as simple as going outside and lying on your kids' trampoline, looking up at the sky, or finding a corner booth at a restaurant and sitting for a few hours with your journal, or maybe renting a conference room at a coworking space and whiteboarding out your ideas. Sometimes changing up your environment helps to break through the limitations and barriers we have set up for ourselves. Here's the challenge: take time to think and to dream. You might even try something really outside of your comfort zone. I love to go to a float tank. This is a sensory deprivation chamber in which you float in salt water—completely in the dark, with no sound—for sixty to ninety minutes. I know it sounds crazy, but some time away from the world in the float tank

---

Wiley, 2018), 130.

often leads to my best ideas. After I get out, I can fill a dozen pages in my journal. Wherever you choose to go, take a journal with you to record all of your brilliant thoughts.

Conduct a 360 Assessment

As mentioned in the introduction, conducting a 360 Assessment was a life-changing exercise for me. There is nothing quite like receiving anonymous, unfiltered feedback from a variety of people in your life. Although I mentioned the negative feedback I received, there were also many positive, encouraging comments. I've used the list of strengths from my 360 Assessment as a filter for which projects to take on and which to pass up. To learn more and sign up for your 360 Assessment, just visit *startwithyourpeople.com/360*.

Your Mirror Manifesto

This brings us to our second exercise to help you discover your who and create your personal purpose statement. I call this your Mirror Manifesto. Each morning, as you get ready for your day, you're eventually going to look in your mirror. Your Mirror Manifesto is a little piece of paper with your ten-step map that you can look at every single day. This is your purpose statement and will give you clarity of purpose throughout the day.

Here's what it looks like before you fill it out.

You know how 1 want to 2?
Well, I help 3 1 4 so they can 5.
I do this by 6 and 7.
This gives me 8.
My clients say I 9 so they can 10.

Here are a few examples from real clients who completed their Mirror Manifesto as part of our coaching process.

Anne:

You know how busy moms want to be fit, even with a busy schedule? Well, I help high-performing, busy moms create a realistic fitness plan so they can feel strong and confident.

I do this by creating a weekly menu and selling nutritional supplements. This gives me a feeling of joy and purpose that I am impacting the health mindset of other women. My clients say I inspire them and help them get fit in less time so they can thrive as a mom.

Tim:

You know how teachers and administrators want to help their students be successful? Well, I help all teachers and administrators implement evidence-based strategies that support learning so they can feel confident in the impact of their work. I do this by teaching workshops, facilitating meetings, and providing coaching. This gives me a sense of purpose, consistent income, and the chance to impact the future generation of students and teachers. My clients say I help them learn and grow so they can become leaders in the field and have a positive impact.

Shelley:

You know how empty nesters want to stay active as they get older? Well, I help amateur empty nest runners keep moving so they can find the confidence and joy in running and feel good about their goals and abilities. I do this by sharing stories, tips, and a calendar of ongoing local running activities on my blog and social media. This gives me a feeling of gratitude and purpose, a generous side income, and positive impact in the running community. My clients say I help inspire them so they can continue to move forward with strength and confidence.

So what about you? Are you ready to create your Mirror Manifesto?

Let's walk through the process step by step.

1. Who Is It That You Want to Serve?

Authors, classroom teachers, business owners?

    I help _____

                    (1)

2. What Does Your Ideal Client Want as a Result of Working with You?

Financial freedom in their retirement years, an organized classroom, a comprehensive life insurance plan, seamless employee benefits?

    They want _____

                  (2)

3. Who Is It Specifically That You Want to Work With within Your Specific Industry?

Female, online, rookie, veteran, private school?

    Write the adjective describing who you want to serve:

_____

        (3)

4. What Do You Help Them Do?

Organize their classroom, manage their finances, coordinate their fundraising plan?

    I help them _____

                (4)

5. What Desired Result Does Your Helping Lead To?

Enjoy teaching again, have confidence each day, have peace of mind, enjoy their job?

    So they can _____

                (5)

6. What Is It That You Give for Free to Your Audience?

Creating a weekly podcast, giving advice about car repair, writing a weekly newsletter, counseling couples online, providing a free download on my website?

I do this by: _____
(6)

7. What Is It That People Pay You For?

Coaching a small group, delivering a keynote presentation, fixing cars, selling life insurance, teaching life workshops?

I do this by: _____
(7)

8. What Is It That You Receive on a Daily Basis as a Result of All That Giving into the Marketplace?

Consistent income, a feeling of gratitude, confidence, purpose?

This gives me: _____
(8)

9. What Is It That Your Clients Say You Really Help Them With?

Save time, gain confidence, clean up their system, be inspired?

My clients say I: _____
(9)

10. What Is Your Ideal Client's Long-Term Goal?

Grow their online business, move up in their career, enjoy location freedom, thrive as a mom?

I help them so they can: _____
(10)

Now is the time to write out your own Mirror Manifesto. Take your answers from the foregoing questions and place them in this paragraph.

You know how _____ want to _____?
             (1)   (2)

Well, I help _____ _____
          (3)   (1)

_____ so they can _____.
        (4)   (5)

I do this by _____ and _____.
        (6)   (7)

This gives me _____.
        (8)

My clients say I _____ so they can _____.
       (9)   (10)

To access the online version of the Mirror Manifesto, with additional video training for free, just visit *mirrormanifesto.com*. At this website, you'll also see other examples to help inspire and encourage you.

Ideas to Consider

- The Mirror Manifesto is the framework for turning dreams into reality.
- Missing pieces in the profitable purpose puzzle keep you from moving forward with clarity and purpose.
- Big dreams without small steps will take you nowhere.
- Your sweet spot is the intersection of knowing what you are good at and finding a way to deliver this goodness to others.
- Get outside your normal zone to look inside yourself.

Actions to Take

- Carefully craft your Mirror Manifesto.
- Discover your who, define your why, and take steps to put your what into action.
- Solicit input on what others see as a strength in you.

How to Grow a Powerful Network

<hr>

I t was one of the most highly anticipated days of my life. For months, I'd been preparing to pitch the vision for our brand-new charter school in front of the state board of education for their approval. It was like going on the TV show *Shark Tank*, having a chance to share my big idea with key investors who could either say yes to my dream or shoot it down. I stayed up every night for a few weeks, refining my presentation for the Louisiana Board of Elementary and Secondary Education. They were the ones with the final authority to let me and my newly formed board of directors open our dream high school, the Mentorship Academy. I had the opportunity to design the charter school application with a small group of supportive community leaders. Now this was our big moment. I practiced my pitch. I went over my slides. I had facts and figures memorized. I was ready.

The stakes couldn't have been higher for me. I had just given my notice, quitting my lucrative job as the director of online programs for a nationally recognized charter school network in San Diego. I'd promised my pregnant wife, Julie, that this move to Louisiana was going to be beneficial for our family. It was the opportunity of a lifetime, and this was my chance to take a big leap.

That morning—October 13th, 2009—was to be my first official day as executive director of the charter school.

The consultant who hired me to run the project had just turned over the reins of leadership to me and my board of directors. I was officially the executive director of the Mentorship Academy. My job was to launch and lead this innovative high school, taking it from an idea on paper to a building full of engaged students and excellent teachers. But first, the state board had to approve our application. Without that approval, we would have no authority to open the school, receive the funding, or move forward. It was one of the biggest days of my life.

As someone brand-new to Louisiana politics, I'd been assured that we were a shoo-in. Approval was virtually guaranteed. All I needed to do was deliver the pitch, and the board would say yes. Quitting my job, moving my family, and taking the risk would all be worth it.

I remember walking through the austere glass doors into the lobby of the W.C.C. Claiborne Building in downtown Baton Rouge, Louisiana, and checking in through security with five members of my board of directors. We were all in our best suits, with proposals in hand. This was our day. We waited outside the hearing room for what felt like hours for our turn to present in front of the state board.

What happened next caught me by surprise. We were called in, and my board chairman was called to the microphone. Before he had a chance to speak, one of the state board members laid into him. "There's no way I can approve your school today," she said.

Uh-oh. This was not a good sign. I remember the words clearly spoken by Linda Johnson, a veteran educator well known throughout the state: "Y'all got to work with the local school district. Y'all need to work it out."

And with that, our pitch was over. We were shell-shocked. I didn't have a chance to say one word. All those hours of rehearsing, all those months of work, meant nothing. The future of the school was in doubt.

I remember walking out of the state government building, with its marble facade and double-paned windows. I looked down at my phone. A text was already waiting from Julie. "How'd it go?" After gathering my emotions, I replied, "There's been a delay, but it's all going to work out." Honestly, I had no idea how it would work out. All I knew was that something had to change.

We canceled our celebratory lunch, and I returned to the office, dejected. Everyone took a half day to regroup, leaving only me, our intern, and a consultant to talk. I slumped into my office chair and overheard the twenty-three-year-old intern say rather matter-of-factly, "You know what the problem is?"

"What?" I asked, still in a daze.

"She burned too many bridges."

The "she" our intern was referring to was the woman who had hired me. The one in charge of assembling the right team and managing the overall strategy. Just for fun, I took out a notebook and said to the intern, "If you were me, which bridges would you repair first?"

Little did I know, this intern was the daughter of one of the most influential business leaders in the region. She knew the real story, and she rattled off seventy names of people I should contact, bridges I should prepare to rebuild. This list included leaders in the community, government officials, and people who worked with the local school district.

As it turns out, the person who hired me had a strategy to go around the local school board and seek approval directly from the state. As a result, many people in the local community felt left out of the process. She had made powerful enemies who helped influence the state board's decision. And this caught everyone by surprise.

The intern explained that the way the project was pushed through had hurt too many feelings. People who had a stake in the success of the school had been pushed aside. My new team *had put the project over people.*

I looked at the long list of names and thought, *If I can get their support, we'll get the approval to open the school.*

I now had a new mission. My job was to rebuild these bridges. Over the next several weeks, I spent every breakfast, lunch, and dinner meeting with someone on that list. At each meeting I asked, "What would you do if you were me?" Asking for their advice humbled me and sparked an immediate connection.

Over dozens of breakfast, lunch, and dinner meetings, I learned the history of the city, gained an understanding of the tenuous relationships in the area, built partnerships that opened doors of opportunity for our students, and developed relationships with future board members.

The local school board acknowledged the work we had done in rebuilding these relationships. Because we reached out to these key stakeholders, they were included in the process. They helped refine the vision. And people support what they help create. The night we presented our pitch to the local school board, the room was packed with supporters from the community. And almost like a miracle, four days after the birth of my first child, our school was unanimously approved. We got the contract we need with the local board, satisfying the state's requirement. And it all happened because we included people in the process.

Since then, the Mentorship Academy has gone on to graduate thousands of students, purchase a multimillion-dollar building, and make a difference in countless lives throughout the community.

This was all possible because we changed our approach to working with people. Reaching out to that list of seventy people was the beginning of this book. The lessons I learned by rebuilding those bridges taught me more than all of my years of studies, including my doctoral degree. People matter. The key difference between a successful company and one that falters is in how a company prioritizes its people.

I've come to realize that everything changes when you put people first.

Relationships have brought me everything I want and probably everything that most people want too. Connection. Belonging. Income. Impact. Community. Purpose. Vision. Interesting work. Fun. Laughter. Adventure.

People have introduced me to incredible experiences, interesting books and resources, delicious foods, exciting adventures, and so much more. People are the key to providing you with next-level experiences and opportunities.

A key skill to develop that saved our school and has led to many of these amazing opportunities is networking. But there are many who feel queasy about networking. Maybe you can relate.

Networking often gets a bad rap. I get it. There are a lot of networking mistakes that people make. Networking can feel like an infomercial or a sales pitch. It takes something beautiful, like building relationships, and turns it into something transactional, like passing out business cards. This lack of true connection can make people feel used, as if they are a means to an end.

As Porter Gale, author of *Your Network Is Your Net Worth*, explains, "The new form of networking is not about climbing a ladder to success; it's about collaboration, cocreation, partnerships, and long-term values-based relationships."[1] Networking is simply relationship building.

---

1   Porter Gale, *Your Network Is Your Net Worth* (New York: Atria, 2013), 58.

Now, I acknowledge that networking can be difficult for a lot of people, especially those who are natural introverts. The idea of meeting new people can be overwhelming and intimidating. But when you think about it, networking is simply building relationships with like-minded people who share similar goals. It's natural to feel queasy about meeting new people, but everything you want comes from a relationship. If you consider yourself an introvert, here are a few tips shared by members of the online writing community I co-run, called hope*writers *(hopewriters.com).*

Confidence is not reserved for extroverts! I remember that I can still be an introvert and get my alone time later to recharge. But when I'm in social situations like conferences, there's opportunities there for connecting, and I can have confidence that the extra socializing will be fruitful and a good investment even if I feel intimidated by it.

—LIBBY

Always, always, ask questions. I'm an introvert and I ask questions, because I prefer to listen to others talk. And listening to others talk creates a mystery. The person talking often feels like they know you well, when they've done all the talking! To connect and show you care about what another person says is worth far more than all those business cards handed out at lightning speed.

—RICHARD

I'm an introvert and find that I'm drained after a lot of social interaction and need alone time to get reenergized. My tip is to pace yourself. If the conference is all day or more than one day, find pockets of time where you can slip away for small periods of time and recharge.

—ERICA

As you can see from these tips, it's possible to develop important relationships even if you are an introvert. By scheduling recharge time, asking questions, and pacing yourself, you too can build a powerful network.

How to Find Your Tribe

As you build your network, you'll begin to discover members of your tribe. Your tribe is a small subset of people within your larger industry. There are people in your space who want to connect with other big thinkers like you. They want to change the industry. They want to explore new strategies. They are ready to try a new way. Connecting with members of your tribe who hold the same values, are headed in the same direction, and are interested in the same topics is incredible. You finally feel like you belong, and it is life-changing. The challenge is to find your tribe. But because of today's technology, it's never been easier to discover your tribe. Here are three ways to find your tribe that have worked for me.

Join an Online Community

Did you know there are free, online groups focused on your industry that you could join right now? In my world of online marketing and publishing, there are scores of groups that are the go-to places to connect with other industry professionals. These groups are free, easy to join, and great places to make connections with people who share similar interests. I'm a member of a few different groups dedicated to the software that I use for our company. I'm a member of several groups focused on connecting with other writers. And I'm also a member of several groups that are focused on my industry in my local area. There are groups available for anything you are interested in as well. Although the tools are always changing, I found awesome groups in Facebook, LinkedIn, and on Meetup.com. As you engage in these groups, you will begin to notice people with whom you really connect. You may be surprised at how opportunities show up as you follow them, answer their questions, and learn about their interests. Once you establish a connection, send them a friend request or a direct message to continue to build your relationship. They might just be the perfect member of your mastermind or someone to bounce ideas off from time to time.

Attend an Industry Conference

One way to discover your tribe is to attend an industry conference. At conferences, you will meet other people in your industry who are passionate about the same things you are. Take Megan, the dental assistant. If she were to attend a dental conference, she would meet other dental assistants who are struggling with the same issues, and she would see them building connections and receiving encouragement. Her tribe reminds her that she's not alone and not the only one facing issues at work.

Host an In-Person Meetup

Another way to discover your tribe is to host a meetup. A meetup is an opportunity for people who share common interests to get together in person. The best place to host a meetup is at a conference because people from your industry are already gathered together.

I host a meetup called the Epic Breakfast Club. It's something I started doing when I attended an industry conference and wanted to connect with some of the speakers and influencers. I called a local breakfast restaurant and reserved their upper room for free. The only thing I had to do was foot the bill for breakfast, which was a few hundred dollars. Think about that—a few hundred dollars to get the most influential people in my industry together in a room. That investment has paid dividends for my business.

But you don't have to pay to have a meetup. You just need to take initiative. You can post a thread in the conference Facebook group or give a shout-out on Twitter letting people know where to meet. Often, when I attend a conference, I will offer to go running with a group of people. There's nothing like sweating together to build relationships.

How to Become a Leader of Your Tribe

Learn

When you close off and decide that you already know everything you need to know, you won't grow. Instead choose to have a growth mindset. There are always new techniques, tools, or trends in your industry. Don't be naive enough to think you know it all. When you hear an idea you haven't tried but it's working for someone else, don't be so arrogant to refuse to give it a try. Learn the strategy and apply it to your situation. New strategies and tactics often lead to new breakthroughs and results.

Execute

To become a leader of your tribe and create next-level results, be fiercely focused on execution. This means implementing those new ideas, systems, and processes. When you attend a webinar, show up for a conference, or read a new book, how are you actually following the advice? An idea without action is just entertainment.

Persist

Never giving up is the key to being successful. Persistence makes the difference. Most of the leaders in my space are in their position because they've outlasted the competition. Yes, of course they learn from others and implement those ideas, but the key difference is that they don't give up. They fail forward. They keep working, no matter what. Their attitude is, "I will be around for the next ten years, so you might as well let me in."

You can establish yourself as a leader in your industry when you make it clear that you aren't going anywhere either. By showing up, serving, and sticking with it, you are bound to succeed. And when you want to give up, when things aren't working quite like you thought they would, keep at it. That is where others give up. But you're not like them. You're a leader of your tribe. You are the difference maker. Your people need you to lead. When it's hard, when it's too much to learn, when it's discouraging, when it's more expensive than you thought it would be, still push forward. Your determination will get you where you want to go.

How I Learned to Network

I was raised in Southern Manitoba, Canada, an insular community where people mostly keep to themselves. Phrases like "growing your network" or "selling your product" can be frowned upon. The community continually reinforced the idea that you should just do good work and be happy making a decent living.

After moving back to the United States after college, I discovered that who you know is much more important than just what you did. I remember one of the first weekends I was in Columbia, South Carolina, visiting my parents' church. I overheard a few people my age recounting their weekend. They had spent the day on the lake, water-skiing, boating, and watching the sunset. Uh-oh. I realized then that I didn't have the skills to invite myself into that opportunity. I remember thinking, *Well, that would be nice, but I won't ever get invited to something like that.* I had these limiting beliefs about what it took to build relationships to open up new possibilities. I had this flawed mindset that said, *If I ask for what I want, that makes me selfish and someone who uses other people.* This didn't sit well with me. I remember walking to the car after church, thinking, *If something is going to change in my life, I am going to be the one who will have to change.* At twenty-one years old, I was going to have to learn the skills and strategies required to find my way into those conversations.

Fast-forward twenty years, and I am known as a great networker. Others in my industry have commented on how I've built an incredible network of amazing people. I truly am blessed by the people I know! When I visit a city like Nashville, I don't have enough time to connect with all of the people I would love to see. I've learned the value of having a robust network of interesting people. And I've learned a number of skills to share with you to help you build your own incredible network.

The Power of Referral Marketing

All the best clients I've ever worked with came as a result of a referral. Someone else loved the work I was doing, and—almost as if out of the blue—I was contacted by a new client asking to schedule some time with me. It was almost effortless, but looking back, I can trace the steps they followed, from awareness to engagement to consideration and finally to a decision. Word of mouth is the most effective marketing. And it all starts with doing well for people. When you do great work, word spreads.

Of course you want to serve your current clients well, and of course you want to deliver on your promise of excellent work. But a great secondary reason to do great work is that great work leads to more great work. Many professionals I've coached lack a clear customer pipeline. My coaching clients are so focused on delivering great work to their existing clients that they don't think about where the money will come from after those jobs are finished.

Instead, "dig your well before you're thirsty." To make sure that you have a steady stream of ideal clients wanting to work with you, you need to create brand awareness, or what my friend Kent Julian calls TOMA (top-of-mind awareness) in your marketplace. People need to see you as an expert who can help solve their problems. When they do, they'll want to work with you. This can often feel like more of an art than a science, but the following three steps can help you develop that expert positioning.

Do Great Work for Your Clients

It's surprising how easy it is to stand out from the competition if you just do what you said you would. People want a quality product or service delivered on time for a reasonable price. When we shortcut quality, deliver late, or charge more than expected, we lose trust and start to lose business.

Create Content That's Easily Shareable

It may be in the form of a testimonial video, a PDF of your process, or perhaps a video series showing the value of the service you provide. Experts today create content. Engaging and helpful content allows happy clients to spread the word about you quickly and easily.

Nurture Your Email List

"The single most valuable asset you have in your online business is your email list," says business coach Marie Forleo.[2] It's important to stay in touch with your potential prospects, letting them

---

2   Marie Forleo, "Cash Machine Transcript," accessed January 15, 2018, at https://programs .marieforleo.com/lessons/website/.

know about the services you offer and the results you're getting for your clients. I recommend having an ongoing conversation with the people on your email list by sending casual, first-person emails on a regular basis. People sign up for your email list on your website and expect to receive regular, helpful content. By building your email list, you will have direct contact with a group of people who are interested in hearing from you. You can learn more email marketing tips at our bonus resources section at *startwithyourpeople.com/bonuses*.

The Dream 100 Strategy

My favorite strategy for identifying the key influencers in your industry and strategically nurturing your relationships with them is called the Dream 100. A concept originating with business strategist Chet Holmes, the Dream 100 is a proven process to serve people by continually staying in touch with them. The strategy works as follows:

1. Identify the key influencers in your industry with whom you want to build a relationship.
2. Create a strategic outreach campaign that nurtures the relationship with those influencers and gets their attention over time.
3. Consistently communicate with them until they do business with you.

If you were a sales representative, creating a list of a hundred people you would love to work with and then strategically nurturing them through a systematized communication strategy and mutual connections would lead to a percentage of them saying yes to doing business with you.

The People Map

Everything you need to be successful in your industry comes from relationships with other people. People are your clients. People are your customers. People open doors of opportunity. Here is some great news, especially if you don't feel like you know the right people or have many connections. Anyone you want to meet is connected to you through a few relationships, or degrees of separation. Do you realize how powerful this can be in your life?

In my industry, every single person I may want to meet is only one, two, or three degrees of separation away from me. I might want to interview the most famous speaker in my industry, but I have not been introduced to her yet. I'm doing all the right things, including following her online, giving her work favorable reviews, and subscribing to her email newsletter, but our paths have yet to cross. However, I know people who know her and can serve as a conduit of connection.

I remember when I was just starting to consider leaving my job at the Mentorship Academy. The school was successful, the team was working well together, and I had found an amazing person to take over the leadership. Traveling to Nashville for a Dan Miller conference, I reflected on the next phase of my career as I listened to a podcast by speaker and entrepreneur Michael Hyatt. On this episode, Michael shared that he was growing his team and looking for someone who loved marketing and understood online education. I thought this would be an incredible fit for my skills and wondered if I would, by chance, cross paths with Michael while in his hometown.

The next morning, less than an hour into the conference, Dan said, "I'm so excited to welcome my special guest, Michael Hyatt." And in walked the very person I had hoped to meet during this trip! I was blown away. While there, I got to know his manager and we hit it off. As a result, Michael and his team became one of the first clients for my brand-new consulting company.

I've often looked back on that interaction and can clearly see the degrees of separation that led to my opportunity to work with Michael Hyatt. First, there was Dan Miller. I had met Dan only one time before, but since I was in his world, I was exposed to Michael. At Dan's event, I met Brian, Michael's manager at the time, and through that relationship I was given an opportunity to work on several projects for Michael. If those connections hadn't existed, I could have spent years trying to get Michael's attention. But because of that newly established connection, there was no longer a degree of separation between us. My work with Michael opened the door to many other clients.

While this connection may seem serendipitous, I now see that you can create a plan. There is a map to your destination. I call it the "people map." This is not a concept that originated with me. I've seen it used in many different contexts. It's such a universal truth that I can't even find the original source, although I would love to give them credit.

Using the people map, you can build a relationship with anyone in the entire world. All you need is an introduction.

1. Start with the end in mind by picking the person with whom you want to connect. This might be the hiring manager for a company, a decision maker for your product or service, or somebody you want to connect with socially. Find one of their social media platforms (my favorite one is LinkedIn, but Facebook works too) and look for a connection.

You

Kathy

As you look through your mutual connections, consider who knows you best and trusts your work. Who can recommend you? What you might find is that you aren't quite ready for an introduction. Instead you might need to build your reputation and your relationships. Put a plan in place and create your people map.

2. If your goal is to connect with Kathy, first you may need to build a relationship with closer connections such as Alicia, David, or Zac. Once you build those relationships, ask for an introduction to Kathy.

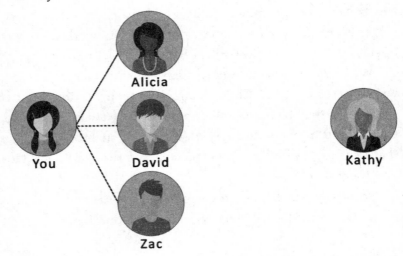

3. If you are not able to get the introduction, look for the next level of connections. Who else might be able to introduce you to Kathy?

Notice that Zac is connected to Kelley, and Kelley is connected to Kathy. How can you serve Kelley? Do great work for her, and after time, ask for an introduction to Kathy.

The people map is a proven, step-by-step process to connect with anyone in the world. Using the people map dramatically expands your network. If you hit a dead end along the way, there's

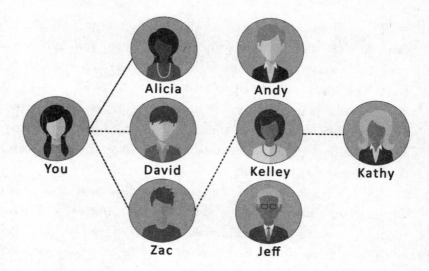

always another way around. You can always connect to someone through one of his or her other mutual connections. The strongest connections are made up of multiple relationships. Just like a strong rope is actually a cord of three or more strands, the best relationship connections happen through many connections. Remember, you're not trying to use people for selfish reasons. You're providing service as you continue to build connections and a reputation.

Let's try an exercise to start building your people map.

Think about a desire that you have right now in your life. How can you clearly define that goal? Who can help you achieve your dream? Think globally. Is it the CEO of your company? Is it an elected official? Is it a spiritual leader?

Put your name in the circle on the left and their name in the circle on the right. Map out the mutual connections. How can you build relationships from yourself to that person in order to create the strongest bond possible?

If you want to appear as a guest on a well-known podcast, start with a lesser known podcast and deliver incredible value. Then ask the host to refer you to another show, where you deliver more value and get referred again. In a matter of months, you're appearing on a well-known show heard by hundreds of thousands of people, because you've delivered value each step of the way.

Use the strategies recommended in this chapter to grow your network by starting with your people.

Ideas to Consider

- Get to know the people around you—from work, your personal life, and so on. Learn how you can help them.
- Remember what your purpose statement—your Mirror Manifesto—is.
- Building a network is essential to helping others and building your business.
- Offering a solution to someone's problem can open doors for you.

Actions to Take

- Identify three ways you can learn more about the relationships you have.
- List three ways you can meet other people so you can begin to network.
- Identify five to seven people to reach out to in order to start your mastermind.

PART 3

PROFIT

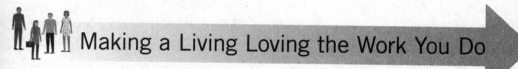 Making a Living Loving the Work You Do

Learning to make money while serving your people can be overwhelming and discouraging.

There is a myth in our culture that conflict exists between impact and income. Either you do the work you love and struggle financially, or you trade the joy of your day for a great paycheck. You can't have both. I say otherwise. You can love the job you have right now and make a decent living. Your people need you to make a profit. Your family needs you to be able to pay for their housing. Your community needs you to fund philanthropic projects. Your church needs you to fund mission trips and weekly expenses. And your future needs you to pay for college, retirement, and some well-deserved vacations.

We've talked about people and purpose; now we're going to focus on the profit. How do you make a living doing what you love? Over the years, I've realized that most of us have a pretty messed up view of money. We blame money for our fights, our feelings, and our fears. But money is a tool to help us live the lives we want. So in this section, I'll first address your money mindset. Then I'll show you a simple path to generating more income without changing your current job.

Finally, I'll show you how to develop expert positioning in your field. You'll learn how to earn a raise as you level up your skills and create demand for your products and services. You'll become well known in your industry, and the compensation will follow.

Serving others by doing what you love is your way to purposeful profit. Let's dive in.

CHAPTER 14

Fixing Your Money Mindset

I have to be honest with you: I didn't want to include this chapter in the book. It's so personal for me. My money mindset is still something I struggle with, and this story shows why.

"I decided I'm not going to go to that conference." That's all she said before going upstairs. Her words broke me. I wanted to argue. I wanted to justify. But the bank account didn't lie. We just didn't have the money. On a whim, I had purchased a conference ticket for my wife, Julie. She'd been talking about this conference for months. So I decided to surprise her and purchase the two-hundred-dollar ticket. But there were a lot more costs involved. By the time we included expenses for travel, accommodations, and food, the investment for the conference was more than twelve hundred dollars. I tried to convince her to put it on a credit card. I told her she deserved it and that she was going to learn a lot and have a lot of fun. I told her we could make it up some other way. But the truth was, we couldn't afford it. Unless we wanted to go into debt, we had to say no. I hated that feeling.

I moped around the house for days. When the weekend of the conference finally came, I couldn't even look at her. I felt like such a failure. All I could think about was how she was missing out. This was not the best way to handle the situation.

I learned much later that the problem wasn't money. The problem was my attitude toward money: my money mindset. For things to change, I knew I had to be the one to change. Over the next few months, I set out to fix my money mindset. I began by looking at money for what it really is—a tool to fulfill my dreams. Not the enemy and definitely not the savior. Just a tool. What I learned over those next few months of exploration changed my life and my business forever.

It's impossible to write a book about people without talking about money. Money is the fuel for so many of the things we want to do in our lives. It funds the opportunities we want to pursue with our people. Almost all of our decisions have something to do with money. But it isn't considered a topic for polite conversation. It's not something we are comfortable discussing openly with our family or our friends. We treat it as something that's embarrassing and selfish. It's no wonder we never have enough! But what if we could embrace a people-first money mindset?

Recently at my church, there was a young woman who said she wanted to be a full-time missionary. She would dedicate her life to moving to a foreign country to reach people she had never met who speak a language she would have to learn. That's incredible. But the problem was, she didn't have enough money to go. I used to feel terrible about these situations. And honestly, slightly annoyed. When I struggled with money, I'd find it annoying that other people were asking for money, even if I believed in the cause. But I've learned that when I work on generating a profit and really delivering for my clients, I can be part of a solution. I love the freedom of being able to help.

Imagine walking up after the service and handing that young woman a check fully funding her ministry, telling her, "You can go right now, because you don't have to worry about fundraising any-more." That is what is possible with a people-first money mindset.

Fixing your money mindset brings clarity and confidence. You charge premium prices for your services. You do the work necessary to get that promotion. You make those extra sales calls to exceed your monthly goals. You bring your best to your everyday work because you know your income matters. It's not just for you anymore. It's for your people. You look forward to the opportunity to bless others through the funds you receive as a result of serving your clients and your company.

Everybody benefits. No one is losing out. When you serve your clients well, you receive abundant income, and when you use that income to bless others, everyone wins. "Pay and profit tell you that you are supplying a need and filling other people's wants," explains author and speaker Daniel Lapin. "They are not the motivation for your work, they are the validation of your work."[1]

Developing a people-first money mindset is essential to serving the people in your life.

Money affects our relationships in profound ways. Money is the solution to so many of our problems. But we treat it like the enemy. It's time for a money mindset that is healthy and balanced.

In reviewing the literature on "money mindset," I've found there are essentially two options: the scarcity mindset and the abundance mindset. The scarcity mindset believes that only one person can succeed: "My success prevents you from being successful." But the abundance mindset sees the world as a place of ever-expanding opportunity: "My success doesn't prevent yours. In fact, it can help inspire yours."

End the Excuses

Most of the excuses I make in my life revolve around money. Money reveals our truest nature. When challenges come, we see who's

---

1   Daniel Lapin, *Thou Shall Prosper* (Hoboken: Wiley, 2010), 333.

been drowning in debt; we see people living paycheck to paycheck. When I was growing up, my dad would say, "An excuse is a reason wrapped up in a lie." If you take radical responsibility for your life and finally own your people-first money mindset, excuses no longer have any place in your life. Whenever I find myself about to use an excuse to justify failure, I remind myself that instead of making up an excuse, I need to take responsibility. There may be other factors that I could use to create an excuse, but there's more that I could have done. If I had really owned it and stepped up, this problem wouldn't exist. Taking responsibility builds trust and allows you to clearly see what to do next. It removes the victim mindset of waiting for other people, hoping they will save you.

Money mindset issues appear at the worst times too. My money mindset slaps me the hardest when it comes to making decisions about going on a family trip, purchasing something for my wife, or signing up for the kids' lessons or sports. It's out of hope that I want to move forward and make a purchasing decision, but fear knocks me back into my place. The pain we feel when we experience a gap between what we want to do and what we can afford is conveniently soothed by a little magic trick, a little white lie known as consumer financing.

Your car is breaking down, so you decide to research what cars are available. You have a set amount put aside, and you know that the dealer has cars within this price range. But they're way in the back, and there's something so enticing about going for a newer model. Instead of looking at the total cost of ownership, you are seduced by the monthly payment. You move toward hope instead of fear, and any doubt is covered by that oh-so-convenient Band-Aid of credit. The problem is, the ecstasy of the new purchase doesn't last very long. After a month or two, the joy of the purchase has worn off, but the reality of the debt sets in. And you have five more years of monthly payments. No wonder we're so afraid to talk about money. It brings up feelings of shame, guilt, and inadequacy.

Giving Up Isn't the Solution

It may be tempting to just throw up your hands and give up. To stop your pursuit of abundance, because it's just too overwhelming. But not having enough money doesn't help anyone. It's impossible for us to provide for our people without income. If we can't feed our family or pay for the roof over their heads, we will be struggling to live free so we can bless others and put them first. But we also have to deal with the opposite end of the spectrum: the greed that comes from the pursuit of wealth, which often turns into the love of wealth and leads to stepping over people and sacrificing relationships to accumulate riches.

Embracing the Three Truths about Money

So how do we develop a people-first money mindset? It comes down to three essential truths. I'm asking you to keep an open mind as you consider each of these.

1. *Money is a tool.* That's all it is. Money doesn't have emotion. Money is not inherently good or evil, though you can use it for either. It's like fuel in your gas tank; you can go farther with it than without it. It's like a hammer; you can use it to build or use it to tear down. It's like a knife; you can use it to prepare a meal or to hurt someone. It's just a tool. You get to decide how it's used.

2. *Money, in some measure, is essential for life.* You need money to accomplish your dreams. This is a hard truth, and I have faced much resistance around this, especially from those in the faith community, who tend to place more emphasis on the pursuit of their mission than on the funding of the mission. I

understand and appreciate their hearts, but you need money to fund the mission. You need money to pay your team, buy equipment for your company, and travel to the places where you are needed. Money is just part of the deal.

3. *Money influences our emotions.* I hesitated to write this last one. I wish it weren't true. But money evokes different emotions in each of us. And if we're honest, usually these emotions are destructive to our relationships. For some, money means guilt. For others, money means grief. For me, money often means validation. When my bank account is full, I feel like a success. When it's emptier than it should be, I feel like a failure. Money brings emotions to relationships, and it can bring out the worst in each of us. I hate to admit that this is true. I hate to admit that the amount of money in my bank account influences my view of myself and my own self-worth. My finances may confine me, but they don't have to define me. Yet it can be a real battle to believe this.

You may be familiar with the concept of HALT, which is a great term to use when you're feeling hungry, angry, lonely, or tired. Usually when my words are unkind and I don't treat people as well as I should, it's because of one of these four factors. When I recognize that I am in HALT, I can simply call it for what it is. I'm just hungry or tired. It's not an excuse for bad behavior, but this self-awareness helps me know where the underlying problem is. Instead of saying unkind words, I can simply recognize that I'm hungry, angry, lonely, or tired and communicate this to the person I am speaking with.

In the same way, when it comes to money challenges, I've also learned to call it for what it is. To say that I'm feeling anxious about the scarcity right now. I'm unsure how we are going to pay the bills. I regret that I have to make this financial decision. It doesn't change reality, but it takes away the emotional power that money often carries. And it brings you closer together with the people in your life. The only way to get your needs met is to vocalize them. I can't teach you to never let money impact your emotions, but I can encourage you not to let it have power over you.

Adopting a people-first money mindset starts with acknowledging these three truths. Money is just a tool, you need money, and money influences our emotions.

The Game of Money

When we learn the rules of a game, we become better players and discover how to win. Many of us are playing the money game without an understanding of how it actually works. If we deny that we need money, we feel guilty for wanting it. Or we give it way too much power, failing to acknowledge that it's just a tool and we are the craftsmen. Money doesn't have control; we can always make choices.

Money Buys Options

The truth about money is that it buys options. I asked my friends on Facebook to share examples of how having more money has provided them with options in their lives. Here are a few highlights.

> For us, it was the option to put our kids in a private school. There we had awesome people pouring into our kids' lives, and our kids received a top-notch education as well.
>
> —BRENDA

In long-term care and senior care, money buys many more options and better-quality care choices.

—SHARON

For me, it allows me to spend my time doing things I enjoy and that I'm good at, and outsource the rest. Money buys flexibility and choice over how I get to spend my time.

—JENNIFER

It's true that money buys options. From school choices to senior care to paying for a little extra help, having those funds can make a big difference. If money buys options, then the opposite is true as well. Lack of money limits options.

I want to acknowledge the elephant in the room. It's the concept of equity, or fairness. Often, that is the argument my email subscribers and coaching clients give me when I talk about why it's a good idea to make as much money as possible. Shouldn't everyone have access to these opportunities? Shouldn't everyone be able to take advantage of these privileges? This is an argument that's almost impossible to adequately address in these few pages, so I'll leave you with this one overarching thought.

It's an often-shared quote from Marianne Williamson: "We ask ourselves, 'Who am I to be brilliant, gorgeous, talented, fabulous?' Actually, who are you not to be? You are a child of God. Your playing small does not serve the world."[2] Our money mindset often serves as a mirror to how we view ourselves. That's why I find this quote inspiring. When you are well resourced, you can bless more people. Having

---

2   Marianne Williamson, *A Return to Love: Reflections on the Principles of a Course in Miracles* (New York: HarperCollins, 1992), 191.

money allows you to choose how you will use it. It allows you to bless even more people. And that's an option worth having!

Overcoming Our Past

So much of the way we feel about money stems from our upbringing and past experiences. We develop a set of beliefs about money based on financial flash points, early-life events that are so emotionally powerful that they affect us well into adulthood. Brad and Ted Klontz explain, in their excellent book *Mind over Money*, that "traumatic experiences create neural pathways in the brain that remain long after the event itself is over."[3] The money mindset you acquired as a child is still affecting your decisions today. It's second nature. And we expect others to have the same views, but they didn't have the same experiences.

My family rarely talked about money when I was growing up. I've struggled with feelings of guilt for achieving a certain level of success, and even considered backing off from pursuing opportunities, because of the strong gravity of my family's money mindset. My grandfather was a bus driver for forty years. My dad was a college professor for forty years. So who am I to try to run a large, profitable company? I have these models to follow. I struggle with guilt, knowing that I want my life, and especially my finances, to look different than past models. I want my family to be worry free when it comes to money. I want to teach my children how to have a people-first money mindset. I want to be a major donor to my church, live debt free, and run an incredible company. No matter how supportive my family is of these goals, my ambitions can feel like a betrayal of the way I was brought up.

If you haven't already, you may experience something similar

---

3   Brad Klontz and Ted Klontz, *Mind over Money* (New York: Crown, 2009), 97.

to this. But be encouraged, your goals and ambitions do not have to mirror those of your parents or previous generations. You cannot change the past, but you can decide not to let it dictate your future. When you start with your people, you can hold your head up high, knowing you are serving the people you were meant to serve, and this is something your family should be proud of!

Money Affects Our Key Relationships

Money is a topic that exposes our deepest fears and our greatest vulnerabilities. Nothing will shut a conversation down and push people into their defensive corners more quickly than talking about money. But friend, we've made it this far. This is important. Stick with me. It's time to address your money mindset. It's affecting your most important relationships.

Marriage. Coming from different families of origin with different expectations about housing, food, entertainment, and vacations can cause tensions in your marriage. It's no wonder financial challenges are often cited as the number one cause of divorce.

Kids. This is one of those time machine moments. I wish I could go back and give myself a warning and let my twenty-five-year-old self know just how important money would be when we started having kids. From the first doctor's visit to whether to get the 3-D ultrasound picture to what kind of crib and baby clothes to purchase, kids cost a lot of money. As they get older, expenses continue to pile up: healthcare, childcare, after-school sports, clubs and hobbies, church retreats, vacations. It all adds up.

Friendships. Around the forty-year-old mark, there are those who start to get even more successful and those who never really make it beyond their starting point. This causes a rift, and so much of it has to do with the mindset we each have about money.

Family. A more recent phenomenon, which has led to the

term "the rubber band generation," is that of paying for kids' college expenses while also paying for elderly parents' senior living expenses. This can stretch even the wisest savers in both directions. It just seems like there's never enough money.

As business coach Mike Michalowicz reminds us, "There is only one way to fix your financials: By facing your financials."[4]

They Need You to Be Successful

At this point, you might be wondering why I'm talking so much about money. After all, this book is supposed to be about people. But here is some hard truth: your people need you to be successful. Your family needs you to get right with money. They are counting on you to step up. The money you earn and save is for them. Housing, food, education—both luxuries and necessities are afforded by the income you generate.

The Future Is a Debt

The future will require your money. It will cost money for you to live and provide for your family. Money goes far beyond today. You will need it tomorrow and every day after that. Randy Alcorn explains, in *The Treasure Principle*, that when "it comes to your money, don't think just three months or three years ahead. Think thirty years ahead."[5] If you're so in debt you don't know where to start, begin with gratitude. What you appreciate appreciates. Be thankful for what you have. It is the beginning of seeing new opportunities.

---

4   Mike Michalowicz, *Profit First* (New York: Penguin Portfolio, 2014), 32.

5   Randy Alcorn, *The Treasure Principle* (Colorado Springs: Multnomah, 2001), 19.

Be a Blessing to Others

If you want to bless others but you're not there yet financially, realize that you have resources beyond money. There are things you have, things you know, and things you are good at. Each of these assets can be used to bless others. I love missionary leader Hudson Taylor's perspective. He wrote, "The less I spent on myself and the more I gave to others, the fuller of happiness and blessing did my soul become."[6] The dollars and other assets you have are tools in your hand that you can use to help other people. Remember that generosity isn't thinking about what you would do if you had the money. Generosity is about who you are and how you are living with what you have right now.

Ideas to Consider

- Money is a tool to be used to fulfill your dreams.
- Money can bring out the best and the worst in us.
- Money affects our relationships with our kids, our spouse, and our extended family.

Actions to Take

- Face your financials. Meet with a financial counselor or a CPA to help you evaluate your situation.
- Sit down with your spouse and discuss a plan with the

---

6   Howard Taylor and Mrs. Howard Taylor, *Hudson Taylor in Early Years* (Manila: OMF, 1988), 121.

four-step process outlined in the spouse chapter to address your money issues.

■ If the scarcity mindset is a particular challenge for you, locate three examples of people who live abundant lives that inspire you to think bigger.

CHAPTER 15

Five Ways to a Raise

S o far in this book, we have focused on how you can effectively serve your people. Now I'm going to show you five
ways of serving the people around you that can increase your
income at your current job.

1. Get to Know Your Industry

When I consult with companies, I'm often surprised by how
employees aren't aware of all the opportunities within their industry. The first way to get a raise is to get to know your industry.
When you do this, you will see opportunities for you to serve.
These opportunities may lead to doing small consulting projects,
serving with your industry association, training others, or even writing articles for an industry association newsletter. And not only do
all of these opportunities improve your resume, but often they also
offer compensation.

2. Identify a Market Gap

The second way to get a raise is to identify a market gap in your industry that you can help solve. This might be a new legal regulation or government requirement, a new problem caused by competition, or a new technology or software application. The market gap lies between the way your company is doing business right now and the way they could be engaging their customers more deeply, which would lead to a brighter future for the company. Consider ways to improve the customer experience, reach new customers, improve order fulfillment, save money on supplies, increase the speed of delivery, or otherwise improve the efficiency of your company.

By identifying a market gap, you position yourself to be the one to solve it. I've seen people get paid just because they are experts in the market gap. There are countless people making a living by working full-time to teach the latest strategies and technology in areas such as social media, marketing, sales, and customer service. They know where the industry is going, and they are paid to tell other people about these trends. You can write training programs, books, and courses, give speeches, and do other things to create content to fill the market gap. These are great ways to supplement your income and serve your company while keeping your current job.

3. Ask for More Responsibility

The best way to get a raise at your current job is to ask for more responsibility. It's better than asking for a raise. What is a project you can take on that no one else is willing to tackle? Where can you provide extra service that will help your company? Perhaps you could coordinate your annual leadership retreat or manage customer focus groups. The budget for these projects is often a different line item than salaries. You are solving a problem and receiving a stipend for your great work.

My favorite way to ask for more responsibility is to participate in a commission structure. Yes, we are talking about sales. No matter where you are in your company, I believe you can help bring in more clients. It's reasonable to receive compensation for new revenue-generating clients you bring in. Here's how you could start this conversation with your direct supervisor.

> Hi, Jane. I have an out-of-the-box idea I'd love to run by you. As you know, I love our company and would love to bring in even more clients. I have a few ideas and was hoping you'd give me more responsibility. Here's my idea: For every new client that I'm able to bring into the company, I would like to receive a small percentage of the revenue. The way you structure it is up to you. I would just love to help out even more, in a way that everybody benefits. Let me know what you think is fair.

At this point, Jane is intrigued. She spends her day managing people who don't want to work, and you're offering to take on more responsibility. Mind blown.

If a team member were to come to me with this offer, I'd find it difficult to say no. You're not giving an either-or. Instead you're saying, "I'm a team player, and it makes sense that I get paid to be part of the team." The commission structure may range anywhere from 3–40 percent. As I'm sure you can imagine, this can be really lucrative. One of my mentors runs an insurance agency. He incentivizes his team members to bring in new clients. If they do, they receive 10 percent of that client's revenue for the first year. Think about that! If the client pays two hundred and fifty dollars a month, that's an extra twenty-five dollars a month, or three hundred dollars a year, just by introducing one of your friends to the company that you already love. It's a win-win scenario for everyone. Your company gets to keep 90 percent of the revenue, and you get a nice little bonus for helping to spread the word.

---

4. Become a Thought Leader

As someone who regularly coaches authors and speakers, I can't help but share how incredible the opportunities are for being a thought leader in our connected economy. People do business with people they know, like, and trust, and the best way to build up the know, like, and trust is by becoming a thought leader. By combining some of the methods we've already talked about, such as getting to know your industry and identifying the market gaps, you can position yourself as a thought leader in your industry. And here's the best part: thought leaders do not have to quit their job! Some of the highest-paid speakers, consultants, and authors I know still have a full-time job. They love their company and feel it's important to continue to stay connected to their industry. It also looks great for their company that they retained such high-caliber talent. The more you grow as a thought leader, the more valuable you become to your employer and your industry.

Here is a four-step plan for becoming a thought leader in your industry.

- *Begin answering questions.* Start participating in your company forums by answering questions there. Go to websites where people ask industry-related questions (such as Quora) and answer frequently asked questions. Remember, what's obvious to you is magic to someone else.
- *Start a blog.* Starting your own website is one of the best actions you can take to become a thought leader in your industry. I recommend you purchase a domain with your name on it (yourname.com) and set up a self-hosted WordPress website.

You can learn more about this process and get it done in less than thirty minutes by going to *NewBlogTonight.com*. Once a week, write a three-hundred- to five-hundred-word article about one issue in your industry. You might write about industry trends, share a tip, answer questions, feature a different product or expert, or create a tutorial.

- *Start an email newsletter.* Stay in touch with people who visit your blog by creating an email newsletter. The tools in this industry are always changing, so check out the latest information at *startwithyourpeople.com/email*. Thought leaders agree: the most valuable asset you have in your business is your email database. It's never too early to start collecting contact information for people you can serve.

- *Speak at industry conferences.* Yes, you probably knew this one was coming, but nothing says thought leader more than being onstage. Speaking at your industry association conference is the best way to demonstrate your credibility to other leaders in your space. And the reality is, your industry needs you to be onstage. They have stages to fill. They have time slots at the conference in which they need somebody to share what's working now. Reach out to your industry association conference planner and volunteer your services. Offer to lead a workshop or a Q&A session, volunteer to help people with registration, and eventually propose teaching a session.

5. Generate Multiple Streams of Income

The final way to get a raise is to recognize that your company paycheck is not the only way you can get paid. Following the tips I've outlined in this chapter, you can get paid your salary, a stipend for helping out your company, and a fee for speaking at industry-related events, plus receive revenue from your website through affiliate offers and advertising and by creating your own products and services such as books, online courses, and coaching programs.

I believe having multiple streams of income is the work model of the future. We will get paid for the value we provide, and that goes beyond a single employer. So serve your company well, and level up your skills by becoming a thought leader in your industry.

Practice

Quick Exercises to Help

You Put People First

Welcome to the practice section of *Start with Your People*. Without application, all the inspiration in the world is wasted. To develop the people-first lifestyle, start with these exercises, each of which takes only a few minutes to implement and a little consistency to master.

Here are the ten exercises.

1. Learn their name.
2. Send thank-you notes.
3. Speak life-giving words.
4. Share your resources.
5. Keep a gratitude journal.
6. Write a review or recommendation.
7. Try what they love.
8. Express gratitude with a gift.
9. Create a morning affirmation.
10. Send birthday wishes.

1. Learn Their Name

Have you ever said, "I'm really bad at remembering names"? Well, my friend, I challenge you to become a gold medalist at learning names. When you say you're really bad at remembering names, what you're really saying to someone is, "I don't care enough to figure out a way to remember the most important word to you—your name."

Here are a few tips for learning names.

- **Repeat their name.** The best thing you can do to help learn a name is to use it often. When you meet someone for the first time, simply say his or her name. "Nice to meet you, Linda." Whenever I am at a restaurant or go get a cup of coffee, I use the name of the person serving me. "Hey, Linda, how are you today?" "Thanks so much, Linda." What I have found is that by using a name three or more times in the context of a conversation, I'm much more likely to remember that person's name.

- **Write it down.** I've found that if I use a person's name three times in my first interaction, I can remember it long enough to get to my phone or a piece of paper and a pen to write down the name.

- **Use apps to your advantage.** When I was in education, there were many school district personnel who interfaced with our schools. I worked with them only on an annual basis, but when I visited the district office, there was a chance I would see them in the hallway. They didn't wear name tags, so I couldn't cheat. Instead I used an app to my advantage. I found a flash card app, went to the district website, downloaded the pictures of the people I would see at the district office along with their first names and job titles, and then I quizzed myself to practice learning their names. This made such a difference, because when I walked into the district office and greeted anyone I recognized by name, it always caught them by surprise and made their day. "Hey, John, how are you doing today?" John would turn around, surprised I knew his name. He might not have remembered who I was. "Hey, it's Brian from the Mentorship Academy. Listen, I just want to thank you for all that you're doing here at the district and the many ways that you're supporting the work that we're doing with our students."

That's the way I started a life-giving conversation in the hallway even though I wasn't there to see John. Don't you think that in a meeting a week or a month or a year later when my name came up, John remembered me? I am sure this tiny gesture made a difference for our school and our students.

Here are a few tips.

- If you're attending a conference, download pictures of the conference team and spend a few minutes with a flash card app, memorizing their names and faces.
- If you are going to a business meeting with people from another company, look them up on LinkedIn or on their company's website. Learn and use their names. It will make a difference.
- Review members of your neighborhood association's Facebook group. Make it a daily habit to learn a few names of people who live in your neighborhood.

Consider other areas of your life where you interact with people on a regular basis. Maybe the bank or the grocery store or the gas station or your church. There are so many social situations in which learning a person's name would be a great investment of your time and energy.

Action Step

- Write down specific locations where you want to learn each person's name.

---

2. Send Thank-You Notes

This exercise will set you apart from almost everyone else in your industry. People love to be thanked. They love to be recognized, and they love to help those who appreciate them. One of the best tools I've found for showing others appreciation is a handwritten thank-you note.

I am aware of my own failing in this area. For years, I wanted to be a thank-you note writer. Even though sending a certain number of thank-you notes per year has made it on my annual goals, I still kept failing . . . until I met Jevonnah Ellison.

Jevonnah is one of those people you never forget. We met several years ago, when we were both speaking at the same conference. The first time I met her—the very first time—she handed me a thank-you note. That's right, a thank-you note upon meeting. It kind of blew my mind. I asked right away, "What do you have to thank me for? We just met." But she's smart; she had done her homework. She said, "We may have just met in person, but I've been following your work for a while. I just want to say how much I appreciate you and all the great work you are doing."

It was memorable. It doesn't take much effort. Where else can a five-minute effort leave a five-year impression? Since meeting Jevonnah, I've seen her implement this strategy in incredible ways. She's a master at follow-up and has inspired many of the strategies listed here.

Recently, I was consulting for a company, and before our first meeting, I looked up the names of the people I would be working with. I packed a box of generic thank-you notes. On my flight, I wrote notes thanking each member of the team for their contribution to the project. I even wrote one to the secretary, thanking her for keeping the lights on and keeping the company going. After we shook hands and got started, I had an opportunity to thank each person by handing them a note. It was a tiny gesture, but I know it left a lasting impression.

Every day, you meet people you can thank. Here are a few reasons to say thank you.

- They did a great job.
- They helped you in some way.
- They answered your question.
- They gave you an opportunity.
- They introduced you to someone.

Every time I rearrange or clean up my office, I always struggle to throw away the thank-you notes I've received. They mean that much to me. With the dozens of times I've spoken at conferences and the thousands of people I've spoken to, I've received only a handful of thank-you notes from attendees. I still have them. A few times I've even reached out and offered to personally help for free, because they expressed their gratitude.

You can do the same thing they did. There's no one too well known, too famous, or too untouchable to appreciate a thank-you note. You can make a world of difference. People support people who are grateful. Sending a handwritten thank-you note is a tangible way to express your gratitude.

- Look back on the last twenty-four hours and consider all the different places you went and all the different people you interacted with. What thank-you notes could you write?
- Send one to your client, saying you're honored to work with her.
- Send one to your boss, thanking him for the opportunity to do work you love.

- Send one to a key vendor, thanking them for partnering with your company.
- Send one to a leader in your faith community, thanking them for investing in you and your family.
- Thank your children's teachers for what they do for your children.
- Thank members of your homeowners' association for all the behind-the-scenes work they do.

Action Steps
- Order thank-you notes online right now.
- Write a list of people you want to thank.
- Message those people and ask for their address.
- Write the thank-you notes and send them.

3. Speak Life-Giving Words

Did you know that your words dramatically impact the results you get? This is true both in business and in life. There is power in the words and phrases we use. Several mentors and friends have inspired me to incorporate more life-giving words into my conversations. Life-giving words inspire and encourage other people.

No matter how much or how little we have, we always have our words. And yet too often, we withhold our life-giving words from those we love the most. Kind, uplifting words are a balm to the soul. Whatever your agenda looks like, I promise, you have time to share some life-giving words of gratitude and encouragement.

Here are some examples of life-giving words.

- "I'm glad to call you my friend."
- "I know things have been hard, and I'm praying for you today."

- "I just wanted to thank you for X."
- "I'm calling to tell you how much I appreciate you."

Life-giving words should not be reserved for those closest to us. Make it a practice to compliment people others fail to notice. While waiting in line in the coffee shop, pay attention to some detail about the person who is going to wait on you, and compliment them. It doesn't hurt to give a compliment. Even something as simple as, "I love coming here. You guys always do such a great job."

Don't be stingy with your life-giving words. Spread them freely. Before interacting with a key person in your life, ask yourself, "What do they desperately want to hear from me?"

- "You really impressed me today."
- "I really love spending time with you."
- "I am so glad you are my son."

So friends, stop holding back your life-giving, life-affirming words.

They are oxygen to the soul, and so many people you know are suffocating. Speak life.

Action Steps
- Text one person right now to tell them what you love about them.
- Open a social media app and send an encouragement video to a friend.

4. Share Your Resources

This exercise may take you a little out of your comfort zone. As I walk around my neighborhood, I notice that my neighbors' garages are always overflowing with too much stuff. But as the saying goes, one man's trash is another man's treasure. The bike your children have outgrown is the perfect size for the kids down the street. The lawnmower no longer in use, thanks to a landscaping service, will benefit the single mother you see daily. The things you have and don't use can bless other people.

Go to your garage or attic and look at the stuff you no longer need. Instead of trying to make a buck by putting it in your community Facebook group or on Craigslist, just give it to somebody. Take the bikes your kids have outgrown, walk to the neighbor's house just a few doors down, and say, "We were cleaning out our garage and thought you guys would like these bikes. What do you think?" They will be blown away. It's a small gesture, it's easy to do, and they will appreciate it. It builds a relationship because you're putting other people first.

Action Step

■ Identify at least one item you don't need and give it to someone who can use it.

5. Keep a Gratitude Journal

Several years ago, when my wife, Julie, was pregnant with our second child, we were going through a difficult season. Extra stress at work combined with the pressure of another pregnancy was leaving us both feeling stretched too thin. I remember getting into the car that morning to go to the office and just feeling like I wished I could tell her how much she means to me. I thought about sending her a text message or leaving her a voicemail, but I was inspired by an idea in Darren Hardy's amazing book *The Compound Effect*, and I decided to give it a try. That very day, on my way home from work, I went to a stationery store and bought a brand-new journal. This was to be a "gratitude journal."

The next morning as I arrived at the office, I left the car running and reached for the journal inside the glove compartment. I wrote a short paragraph telling Julie what she means to me and how much I love her. I kept the journal in the glove compartment.

Every day for the next sixty days, when I arrived at work, I got a reminder on my phone to write in the journal. Over time, I began to fill up that journal.

When our daughter was just a few weeks away from being born, just around Thanksgiving, I gave Julie the journal. She told me it was the best gift she had ever received. She had evidence that I had been thinking about her, and it showed how grateful I am for her.

I began to see opportunities for gratitude each and every day, even after I gave her the journal. I began to vocalize more how much she means to me, because I had created the habit of recognizing gratitude. This strategy can literally change your marriage, just as it improved not only my marriage but also my mindset about my wife and my life.

Action Steps

- Find a journal you've never used or buy one.
- Put it in a place where your spouse or partner is not going to find it—under the car seat, in the glove box, or even in a secure desk at work—and set a time each day when you can write in it. It doesn't take more than a few minutes.

As you write in the journal each day, begin to anticipate the day you will give your spouse or partner the journal: a birthday, Christmas, Thanksgiving, or an anniversary.

6. Write a Review or Recommendation

If you have a good experience with a book or a business, write a review. Reviews help customers make informed decisions, but they mean even more to the business owner. If you ask business owners what they want more than anything else in the world, they'll likely say more sales. They want to have a company that consistently generates profits and allows them to focus on what they love to do. For a restaurant, that means new patrons checking out the ambience and the food. For a service-based business, that means engaging new clients and having them sign up for packages. For an author, that means selling more books.

People need reviews. When it comes to sales and marketing, one of the most important assets you can have is a list of customer testimonials. Potential customers want to know whether the product or service is going to work for them. Authentic customer testimonials are a powerful way to encourage potential customers to make an informed buying decision.

Think about organizations and companies you frequent. Here are some review ideas.

- Is there a local business that does an amazing job creating printed materials for your company?
- Do you have a home repair company that does great work, rain or shine?
- Do you have kids? You can review your child's school. Type the name of the school in your web browser's search field along with the word *review* or *rating*. You will likely find a few websites with reviews of that school. If it's a great school, why not give back by leaving a positive review?

There are many review sites around. One I frequently use is

Yelp. Anytime I'm thinking of going out to eat in a new city, the first thing I do is check Yelp. I want to know what people are saying about which restaurant I should go to. Let's start there.

Action Steps
- Open Yelp (or a similar site) on your computer or your phone.
- Find a local restaurant you love and give it a good review.
- If you love this book so far, would you take a minute to leave a review there? It will help more readers discover this book. Thank you!

---

7. Try What They Love

Another people-first exercise is to try what they love. Maybe for the last few years, you've made fun of something that someone important to you loves—a certain kind of music or a sport or a TV show. For just today, try what they love. Give it a chance. Suspend judgment for one day. Try to keep your opinion, if it's negative, to yourself. Instead try to figure out why, specifically, the person important to you likes that particular thing.

If your team likes to go to a certain restaurant, invite yourself along one day. "Hey, can I join you guys for lunch? I see you always have those kinds of sandwiches, and I've never tried them." It will mean a lot to them. It shows you are trying, and that really matters. And here's the surprise: you might actually enjoy it. Most of the things I love today are a result of a recommendation. Instead of closing my mind to trying something new, I open up to the opportunity. If I love and respect someone, there's a chance I might like the thing they like. Give it a shot. Love what they love, even if it's just for one day. Your effort alone will mean a lot to them.

Action Steps

- Find something that someone important to you loves and take an interest in it.
- Give it a chance and try it.
- Figure out why they love it; try to see it from their perspective. You might find you like it too.

8. Express Gratitude with a Gift

Gratitude. It's so simple that you can easily forget to express it. But gratitude changes everything.

I love to open doors of opportunity for people. When my coaching clients win, I win. When the organizations I consult with win, I win. When my readers get results that help them win, I win. I love to support and encourage people. But there's one thing they can do after I've helped, after I've inspired, after I've encouraged them to move forward: turn around and say thank you.

Gratitude is bigger than saying thank you to people who have helped us. It's an attitude. It's a lifestyle. When you see the world through the lens of gratitude, opportunities open up, because people want to help you. You start to see possibility instead of scarcity, and results, not roadblocks. And you begin to connect the dots. You see something and think, *My friend _____ would really appreciate this*. An attitude of gratitude inspires you to appreciate people who have invested time and effort in you and thank them in ways that are especially meaningful to them. That's key. It's not giving them a five-dollar coffee shop gift card or a pen engraved with your corporate logo and thinking, *There, that's enough*. Did something stand out to you during a recent interaction? A simple handwritten thank-you note conveying that memory or impression is especially meaningful. (Has there ever been a time when you were disappointed to receive an unexpected handwritten thank-you note?) And when it's accompanied by something that captures the spirit of your interaction or the essence of your relationship, it packs a memorable punch.

In his excellent book *Giftology: The Art and Science of Using Gifts to Cut through the Noise, Increase Referrals, and Strengthen Client Retention*, professional gift consultant John Ruhlin explains the power of gift giving. He refers to a framework I highly recommend. Here's a quick synopsis.

1. Give what people want, not what you want them to have.
2. Use gifts to build relationships.
3. Give gifts without expectation.[1]

If you do these three things, you can open up amazing doors. But that's not why we do it. We give gifts because we're truly appreciative. We simply want to express our gratitude. "You mean a lot to me. I'm thankful for you. Here's something I thought you would enjoy."

Action Steps

- Think about your recipient. What has meaning to them?
- Think beyond the gift to its timing and its delivery method. Sometimes the when is as significant as the what. Can you do something unique with packaging, a personalized note, or the timing of the gift's arrival?
- Consider giving gifts at times they're least expected. Your gift will stand out more if it's not one among many.

---

1   John Ruhlin, *Giftology: The Art and Science of Using Gifts to Cut through the Noise, Increase Referrals, and Strengthen Client Retention* (Austin: Lioncrest, 2016), 90.

9. Create a Morning Affirmation

This exercise is a secret hack in the world of leaders. We need regular reminders to focus on what's important and push through the challenges we'll face. A tool I use to start each day is a daily affirmation. This is a written statement reinforcing who you are and who you are becoming.

Here's how to create an affirmation.

1. Think about who you want to become and how you want to treat your people.
2. Write this out as a positive statement. Have the written statement available for daily review.
3. Bonus: Record an audio version or hire someone to record an audio version of the affirmation. I paid someone thirty dollars on upwork.com to record my affirmation in MP3 format so I could listen to it daily. When I wake up, it's the first thing I listen to. It's one of my favorite ways to defeat the grumpies in the morning. It serves as a reminder of who I am and why I'm here.

Here is a portion of my morning affirmation.

Brian sees every day as an opportunity. He is not perfect, but he is quick to apologize and to ask for forgiveness. When someone wrongs him, he gives them the benefit of the doubt by putting them first and forgiving them even if they never ask for forgiveness. He is patient with the people in his life and the journey they are on. And he is intentional. Brian starts his day focused on deepening and living out his faith. He loves his wife, Julie, intentionally, puts her first, and treats her with kindness. Brian is an intentional and loving father. He loves and teaches his kids according to the way they are made. Brian knows that his words have deep and lasting meaning and that his kids are constantly watching his actions and modeling their lives after his example. When it comes to relationships with his team, his friends, and others he interacts with, Brian brings light into a room and inspires others to live their best life no matter what they're struggling through or facing. He is an encourager to the discouraged, an inspirer to the hopeless, and a friend to everyone he meets. Brian knows that the days are short. He has such a limited time to make such a big difference. So he does not get bogged down in worthless conversations and empty pursuits. Instead he presses on, rising above the noise and distraction of our mediacentric culture, reviewing his long-term life goals daily.

See how powerful this is? My morning affirmation is the secret to my positive outlook and never-quit attitude. I highly recommend you try it for yourself.

Action Step

- Create a written morning affirmation and consider an audio recording.

10. Send Birthday Wishes

Thanks to social media, we now know when it's someone's birthday. Every day, if you log in to your favorite social media platform, you will see a list of all your friends who are celebrating birthdays today or will be in the near future.

Most people simply visit their profile and type, "Happy Birthday." Why not go above and beyond? Instead take out your phone and record a ten- or twenty-second video message wishing them a happy birthday, and name one thing in specific you appreciate about them. Then send this video message directly to that person.

Send the birthday greeting the day before their birthday. I love doing this. Not only will it show that you put extra time and thought into it, it will help your birthday message stand out from the crowd of messages they will receive on their birthday.

Action Step

- Log in to your primary social media account, find the birthdays for your people, and note them on your calendar.

Tomorrow Morning

Now that you've made it all the way through the book, I want to talk about tomorrow morning. Every day is a new beginning. A new opportunity for change. I want to challenge you: instead of putting this book on the shelf or passing it on to a friend, apply it starting tomorrow morning.

From the moment you wake until the moment you go to bed, you can start with your people.

We're going to start with the morning. How you face the morning is how you face your day. The first hour is the rudder. It sets the direction for the rest of your day. When you get pulled off course, it can be difficult to remember to put people first. So the goal of this final challenge is to be intentional with your morning routine. My friend Crystal Paine, founder of Money Saving Mom, explains, "How you approach your day when you get up each morning can have an effect on not just your entire day—but your entire life."[1]

To start with your people, we're going to begin with your morning routine.

Your morning routine lasts from the time you get up until the time you start your work. In his five-year study of self-made

---

1   Crystal Paine, "15 Things You Can Do Each Morning to Make Your Day More Successful," Money Saving Mom, March 5, 2013, https://moneysavingmom.com/15-things-you-can-do-each-morning-to-make-your-day-more-successful.

millionaires, author Thomas C. Corley found that nearly 50 percent of them woke up at least three hours before their workday began. But the average person wakes up less than two hours before the beginning of their workday.[2]

However, it's not just when you wake up that makes a difference. It's what you do when you are awake. Creating your ideal morning routine that puts people first will give you the right mindset for the day.

With this in mind, here are seven tips for developing your morning routine.

1. *Create a plan.* Start with your ideal morning. Write it out. What do you wish to accomplish by the time you get into the office? Create a schedule in five- or ten-minute chunks of time. Literally write it out. "Wake up at 6:00 a.m. Finish showering by 6:15 a.m. Dressed by 6:30 a.m."

2. *End your routine with something you enjoy.* Use this enjoyable activity as a buffer between your commute and arriving at the office. What do you wish you had more time for? Taking a walk? Enjoying a cup of coffee? Writing? Reading? Listening to your favorite music? This will help motivate you to complete your routine on time so you have time to enjoy that activity. It will also serve as a buffer if you need to arrive at the office early.

3. *Your morning routine starts the night before.* Once you have a well thought out morning routine, consider what you can prepare ahead of time. Before I go to bed, I have three tasks I complete to get ready for the day: (a) set out my clothes; (b) place any items I need to take with me in a special spot; (c) write out my list of goals for the morning.

---

2   Ars Technica, "How Early Do You Wake Up before Arriving to Work?," modified May 25, 2018, *https://arstechnica.com/civis/viewtopic.php?f=23&t=1229759.*

4. *Consider the compound effect.* If you do just 7 push-ups a day consistently each morning, that adds up to 2,555 push-ups a year. Positive routines add up to positive long-term results, and negative routines add up to negative ones. It might just seem like a morning doughnut, but consider the impact of those extra calories over the course of an entire year. Start small with positive habits in a healthy direction, and you will see positive long-term results.

5. *Carpe diem as you commute.* Use the time in your car on the way to work to get inspired. Negative music, news, or talk radio doesn't lead to an improved self. Consider instead inspirational music, an uplifting audiobook, or a motivational podcast.

6. *Reflect on your values.* Remember each morning the reasons you are going to work: to generate income in order to provide for your family, to make an impact on your community, and to encourage those around you. This reminder will help you push through the most difficult of mornings. You might even consider printing out a statement about why you go to work, placing it in your car, and reviewing it before you leave your driveway each morning.

7. *Take some time for yourself.* Set aside some time each day (at least thirty minutes) to be alone. Select a time when your mind is fresh and you can be free from distractions. Use this time to do two types of thinking: directed and undirected. For directed thinking, review a major problem you face. In solitude, your mind will study the problem objectively and lead you to the right answer. For undirected thinking, just let your mind select what it wishes to think about. Undirected thinking is helpful in self-evaluation. You can get down to very basic matters like, "How can I do better? What should be my next move?"

If you follow these tips, here's what will change for you. Your kids will be less reactionary. You'll be less irritable. Your spouse will be more appreciative. And your coworkers will begin to notice a difference. Start with your morning routine, and the rest of the day gets better.

I want to thank you for taking this journey with me. As we finish our journey together, I want to point you to a few additional resources. First, the bonus section that follows includes tips for email communication and a description of my favorite personality tests. Second, you can find additional tips and resources in our online bonus section at *startwithyourpeople.com/bonus*. And finally, there's an opportunity at that site for you to share your best people-first ideas. So hop over there and let's connect.

1. Three Emails Every Company Needs to Send Today

One of the ways you can put people first, especially in your company, is through your communication. As someone who has sent millions of emails on behalf of my clients, I have learned a lot about emails and email marketing. So in this bonus section, I will share three emails every company needs to send today. These three emails are responsible for the majority of our revenue and have set us apart as a people-first company.

Email 1: Assessing Needs

The first email is all about figuring out the needs of your clients. This is a customer-facing email that we've sent across multiple brands. It has made such a difference in the way we produce and market our products and services.

Example
Subject: Where are you stuck?

> [Customer name],
>   I was thinking about you and how grateful we are to be connected because of our work together.

> In our team meeting today, we were wondering where you might be stuck.
>
> Just hit reply and let us know.
>
> Here to serve you.
>
> Your Name

Explanation

The reason you should send this email no matter what industry you're in is because it brings you closer to your end user. Your customers will tell you where they're stuck. And people pay for the pain to go away. Ask them where they're stuck and they'll tell you. My favorite way to get this information is to simply allow somebody to hit reply. Ideally, you're sending from your individual email account and not from the company newsletter email address. When in doubt, always be more personal. Personal makes the difference.

What Do You Do after Sending This Email?

It's important to write back to your people when they respond. Carefully read their replies and think about how they are stuck, then provide your recommendation based on what they said. If you run a dental office and they say they're stuck when it comes to picking out the right kind of toothpaste, then write back and tell them your favorite toothpaste and how they can purchase it. It's really simple. You ask people questions, they answer, and you respond.

What if a thousand people respond? That is a great problem to have. No matter how big or small your company is, wouldn't it be incredible if you had your customers speaking directly to you? Then you would know tangible ways you could help them.

Secret tip: One of my favorite reasons for using the "where are you stuck?" email is being able to use the words they share for text copy on your website and in your future emails. If they say, "I'm stuck trying to figure out which kind of toothpaste I should use," then your next email newsletter or blog post or Facebook post could be, "Are you stuck trying to figure out which toothpaste you should use? In this video, I will explain which toothpaste you should use and why."

See how easy that is?

Email 2: Feedback about Your Company

If the first email is asking where your customer is stuck, the next email is focusing on where your company is stuck. Think of this as a 360 Assessment for your company, providing insight much like your 360 Assessment does.

Example

Subject: Tell us the truth [or, How are we doing?]

> Hey, [Customer name],
>
> We're having a company retreat in a couple weeks, and we really want to improve the way we serve you.
>
> Hit reply and let us know how we can do better.
>
> We promise we will read your reply and try to implement your suggestions.
>
> Thanks.

Why Send This Email?

Your most engaged customers and clients will tell you how to make things better. Listen up! The things they say should be on your goal list for the following year. Often, the challenges they bring up are very easy fixes. When we create a business, we think everything is intuitive to our people, but often it's not. Sometimes really simple things, like making your phone number more prominent on your website or improving the way you answer the phone, can dramatically affect the way customers interact with your business. You don't know until you ask.

When people tell you how to improve, go through their responses and consider ways to address their concerns. Some of the best innovations you'll ever create as a company will come from this email.

Email 3: Products We Love

A great way to provide value for your people is to introduce them to products you love. When done right, this can also increase your company's bottom line. Many companies have ways you can become an affiliate referral partner. By recommending someone else's product or service, having registered as an affiliate, you'll receive a unique link for your company. Anytime someone purchases through that link, you will receive a percentage of that sale. By thinking beyond your own products and services and addressing the needs of your customer, you are putting your people first.

Right now, a large percentage of the revenue I receive on a monthly basis is a result of recommending products and services I love and use. I get paid a commission every time people click on my link and purchase.

Recommending another person's product or service helps strengthen your relationship with your customers. Your customers benefit from the results they receive from the product or service. Additionally, you're also encouraging and helping the vendor who created that product or service, by increasing their bottom line. Affiliate marketing, when done right, is truly a triple win. It's a win for you, a win for your customers, and a win for the vendor.

Example

Subject line: Check out this X [or, If you're struggling with X, check this out]

> Hey, [Customer name],
> Many of our clients like you struggle with X.
> So our team put together a list of tools to help you with X.
> Here are three of our favorites we know you will love.
> Click the link to learn more and to check them out.

Here's a specific example. Let's say you are a Realtor, and you have an email list of people interested in selling their homes. These people are struggling to figure out the right time to move, so the email will be focused on moving.

Subject: My favorite tools before you move

> [Customer name],
> Are you struggling to pick the perfect time to move? My team and I got together and created a list of our three favorite resources to help you make that tough decision.
> Click the link to check them out.

Side note: Links could point to books, videos, podcast downloads; they don't have to go to purchasable content. You are showing people you are a valuable resource for the product or service they are looking for.

For more ideas on communicating with your clients, visit *startwithyourpeople.com*.

2. Four Core Personality Tests

Investing time and effort to better understand your people is always worthwhile. There are four tests that will give you a well-rounded view of the people in your life. Here are my four favorite resources.

1. Love Languages = how to give and receive love from your partner
2. Enneagram = how you see the world
3. Kolbe = how you instinctively take action
4. StrengthsFinder = what makes you gifted (your superpowers)

1. Love Languages

There's a great book, *The 5 Love Languages: The Secret to Love That Lasts* by Gary Chapman. You've likely heard a few of the concepts before. Each of us has one of the five love languages as our primary way of giving and receiving affection. The five love languages are:

1. Words of affirmation
2. Quality time
3. Receiving gifts
4. Acts of service
5. Physical touch

Think about it this way: You want your spouse to support your dreams, but she is feeling unloved. She needs you to spend quality time with her, but your side business is taking all of that time. You think giving her gifts makes up for the time away, but you are not speaking her love language. She is feeling unloved and will see your dream as a threat.

There's a love language test online at *www.5lovelanguages.com* to help you figure out your love language. Just knowing that my wife's love language is acts of service means that all the gifts in the world, all the hugs in the world, and all the kind words in the world are not as valuable as me putting away the dishes and cleaning up the kitchen. Emptying the dishwasher is worth a lot more to her than all the words I could possibly say. Your spouse has a love language. Your job is to learn to speak your spouse's love language.

2. Enneagram

There is an ancient personality test called the Enneagram. I know, it sounds a little bizarre, and I was once very skeptical too, but it has proven to be revolutionary in my relationship with my wife, Julie, and in the relationships of other couples I know. Understanding the Enneagram has changed the way I see the world. It has also helped me understand how Julie sees the world. You can even use the Enneagram at work to better know your team.

I have found the concept of the driving question to be the most powerful way to empathetically consider how another person views the world. My friend Ian Cron explains in a video I created for his Facebook page, "In each of our hearts there lives a question that profoundly influences how we see the world and live our lives. We may not know this question exists because it operates beyond our awareness, but it's the unseen motivation that drives our behavior and often determines our ability to find peace and satisfaction."[1]

According to Ian, the nine questions, with their corresponding Enneagram types, are as follows:

Type 1: The Reformer. Why is there a voice in my mind that mercilessly criticizes my behavior and the behavior of those around me?

Type 2: The Helper. Why do I feel driven to meet everyone else's needs while ignoring my own?

Type 3: The Achiever. Why do I believe the world really loves and values only people who achieve success and win the admiration of others?

Type 4: The Artist. Why do I feel like there's something flawed or missing in my essential makeup that prevents me from enjoying the happiness and sense of belonging that others appear to enjoy?

Type 5: The Investigator. Why does the world seem so intrusive and draining that I frequently have to withdraw from it to gather information and knowledge and recharge?

---

1   Ian Cron, "Do You Know Your Question?," Facebook video, 5:24, posted March 2017, https://www.facebook.com/IanMorganCron/videos/10154830812460630.

Type 6: The Loyalist. Why am I always imagining and planning for worst-case scenarios, even when my life's going great?

Type 7: The Enthusiast. Why am I always dreaming up and planning exciting adventures, thinking about fascinating ideas, and imagining a future filled with unlimited possibilities?

Type 8: The Challenger. Why do people tell me I'm confrontational, domineering, and argumentative to the point they feel intimidated by me?

Type 9: The Peacemaker. Why am I so deathly afraid of conflict that I do anything to avoid it?[2]

So which question most resonates with you? Which most resonates with the people in your life? These questions will help you figure out your Enneagram type. You can also take a test here: *startwithyourpeople.com/bonus.*

3. Kolbe

A third personality profile I love is the Kolbe Index. Basically, this test can help you figure out how you instinctively take action. Are you more of the fact finder? Or are you a quick start? Understanding this can help you and your team to be on the same page. This knowledge can benefit your marriage as well. Both at home and at work, you'll have projects to tackle and tasks to complete. Knowing how you and those around you approach those tasks can help improve both communication and project completion. Learn more at *kolbe.com.*

4. StrengthsFinder

Often, it's easier for us to recognize areas where we are weak than to work in our strengths. But here's the truth, friend: you have

---

2   Ian Cron, "Do You Know Your Question?," Facebook video, 5:24, posted March 2017, https://www.facebook.com/IanMorganCron/videos/10154830812460630.

strengths that make you awesome. The Clifton StrengthsFinder test will identify your strength DNA, helping you know exactly what kinds of tasks and projects you should be working on and where you should bring in a team member with complementary strengths. I regularly refer to my top five strengths to know where I am going to thrive, and my bottom five to know what I should avoid. A quick online test, and you'll discover your top five strengths. You can learn more about the Clifton StrengthsFinder test at *gallupstrengthscenter.com*.

A Quick Favor

I want to ask you for one last favor as we wrap up this book.

If you've gotten any value from *Start with Your People*, could I please ask you to share a review of this book?

You go to *startwithyourpeople.com/review* to leave your honest review.

This will help more people discover the message of this book, and it truly means a lot.

Thanks again.

—Brian

Acknowledgments

First, I want to thank you. Thank you for not just reading this book but applying the principles to your life and work. Never forget that you have a message to share and an audience to serve. Just start with your people. If I can ever be of assistance, don't hesitate to reach out. Email me at brian@briandixon.com. I'm so grateful for you.

Bringing a book to life is truly a team effort. Thank you to Lisa Jackson and the team at Alive Literary for championing this message. To Stephanie Smith and the incredible team at Zondervan, including Alicia, Robin, David, Tom, Matthew, and Keith. Thank you for your tremendous work and support along the way.

To Dan and Joanne Miller. Thank you for showing me that profitable purpose starts with people.

To Julie and my home team, including Ryland, Emmaline, Hudson, Larry and Linda, George and Annette, and of course Nanny.

Huge debt of gratitude to those who helped shape the book in the early stages, including Denae Armstrong, Amy Chapman, Daniel Decker, Tim Willard, Hope Dover, and all of the editing interns and book launch team members. The full list with links is available at *startwithyourpeople.com/team*.

To the members of hope*writers and my friends Emily P. Freeman and Gary Morland.

To the friends and colleagues who continue to challenge me to level up, including Amy Porterfield, Ruth Soukup, David Taylor, Ray Edwards, Henry Hays, Jamal Miller, Zac Jiwa, David Ogwyn, Kevin Conklin, Ryan Levesque, Shane Freeman, Sheila Murphy, Chad and Myquillyn Smith, Kent Julian, Ryan Holiday, Jeremy and Amanda Bacon, Alicia Mundt, Ben Arment, Jennifer Allwood, Ryan and Stephanie Langford, Jevonnah Ellison, Michael Hyatt, Kary Oberbrunner, Mike Kim, Stu McLaren, Chandler Bolt, Jonathan Milligan, Mark Timm, Pat Flynn, Cliff Ravenscraft, Jeff Goins, Pete Vargas, Rachel Miller, Susie Moore, and Rhéal Pelland.

I am grateful for each of you.

Resources

My team and I are here to help you incorporate the strategies shared in this book into your life and work. Here are the resources we offer.

Courses

A great next step is to sign up for one of our online learning experiences. Take a thirty-second quiz at *startwithyourpeople.com* to discover a course that perfectly suits you.

Coaching

Looking for a more personalized experience? Sometimes you need someone else to come alongside you and offer individualized feedback and guidance. Learn more about my coaching for teams and individuals at *briandixon.com/coaching*.

Speaking

I love speaking at conferences to help inspire, educate, and encourage your attendees, helping them to see that their people matter. Check out example speaking videos and booking information at *briandixon.com/speaking.*

One Last Thing

If you got anything out of this book, if you took notes, if it shifted your thinking or inspired you at all, I'm hoping you'll do something for me.

Give a copy to somebody else.

Ask them to read it. Let them know what's possible for them. If they really value their goals and dreams over their excuses, we need them. We need you.

Please spread the word.

Thank you!

For gift ordering, visit *startwithyourpeople.com/gift.*